Alexander Graham Bell

SADDLEBACK
EDUCATIONAL PUBLISHING

Saddleback's Graphic Biographies

SADDLEBACK
EDUCATIONAL PUBLISHING
www.sdlback.com

ISBN-10: 1-59905-213-X
ISBN-13: 978-1-59905-213-7
eBook: 978-1-60291-576-3

Printed in Malaysia

21 20 19 18 17   8 9 10 11 12

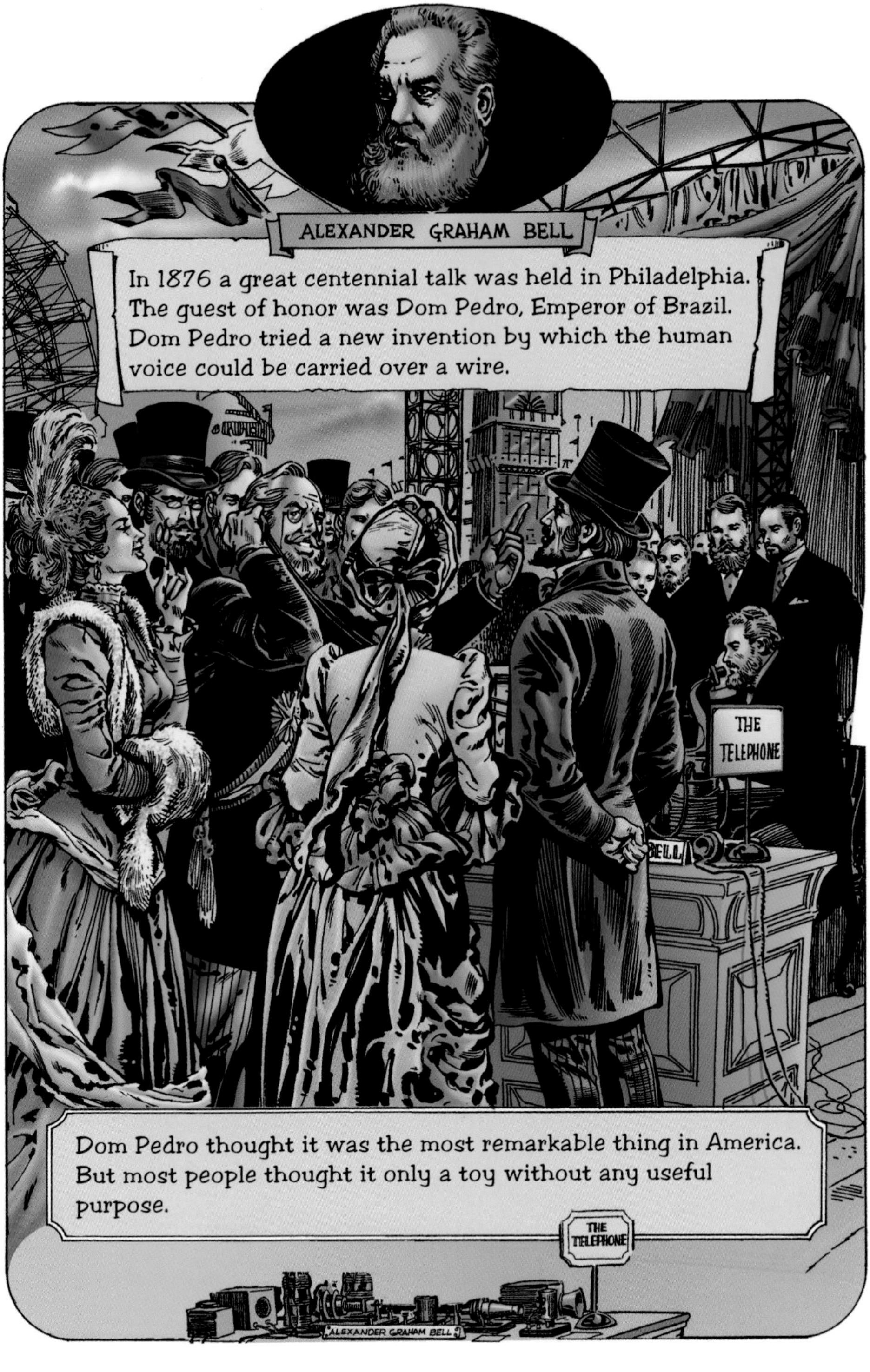
ALEXANDER GRAHAM BELL
In 1876 a great centennial talk was held in Philadelphia. The guest of honor was Dom Pedro, Emperor of Brazil. Dom Pedro tried a new invention by which the human voice could be carried over a wire.
THE TELEPHONE
BELL
Dom Pedro thought it was the most remarkable thing in America. But most people thought it only a toy without any useful purpose.
THE TELEPHONE
ALEXANDER GRAHAM BELL

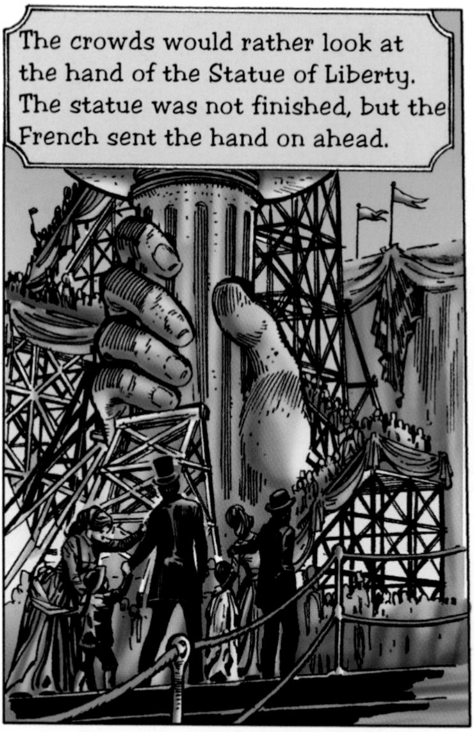
The crowds would rather look at the hand of the Statue of Liberty. The statue was not finished, but the French sent the hand on ahead.

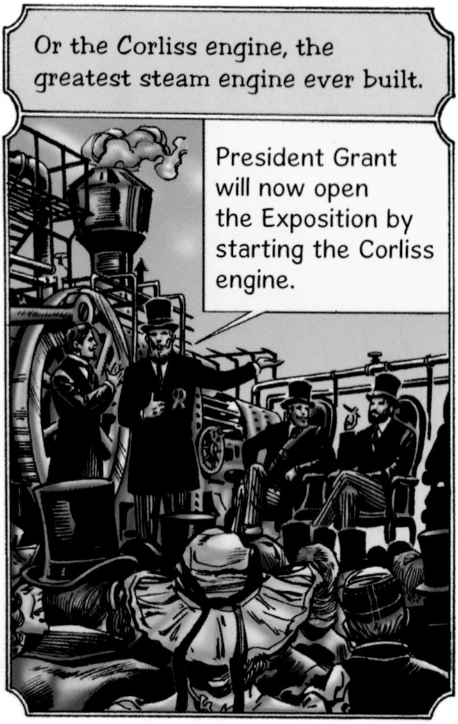
Or the Corliss engine, the greatest steam engine ever built.
President Grant will now open the Exposition by starting the Corliss engine.

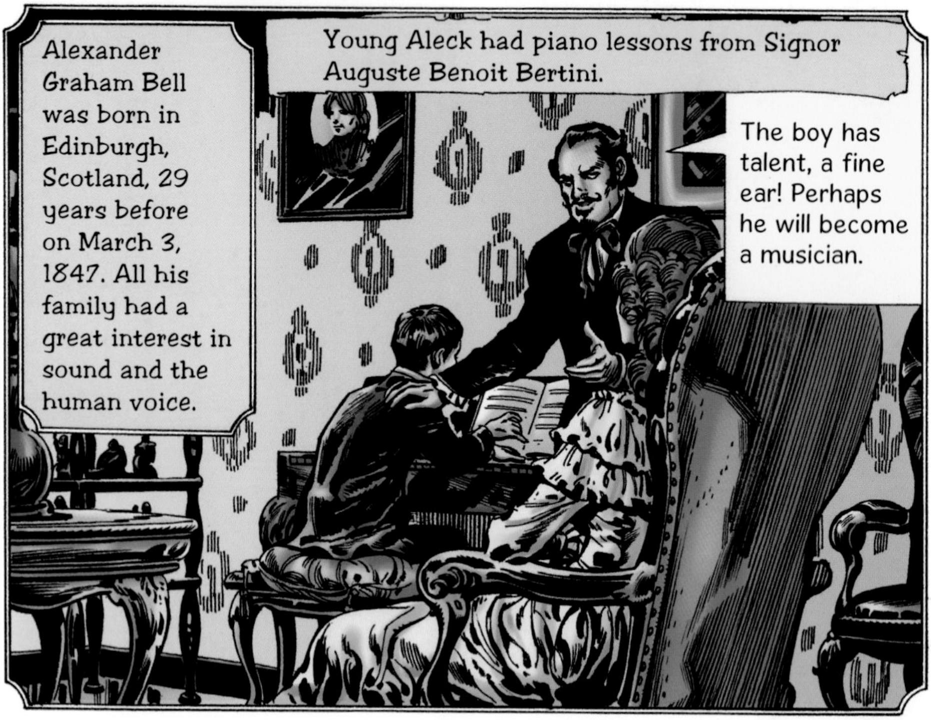
Alexander Graham Bell was born in Edinburgh, Scotland, 29 years before on March 3, 1847. All his family had a great interest in sound and the human voice.
Young Aleck had piano lessons from Signor Auguste Benoit Bertini.
The boy has talent, a fine ear! Perhaps he will become a musician.

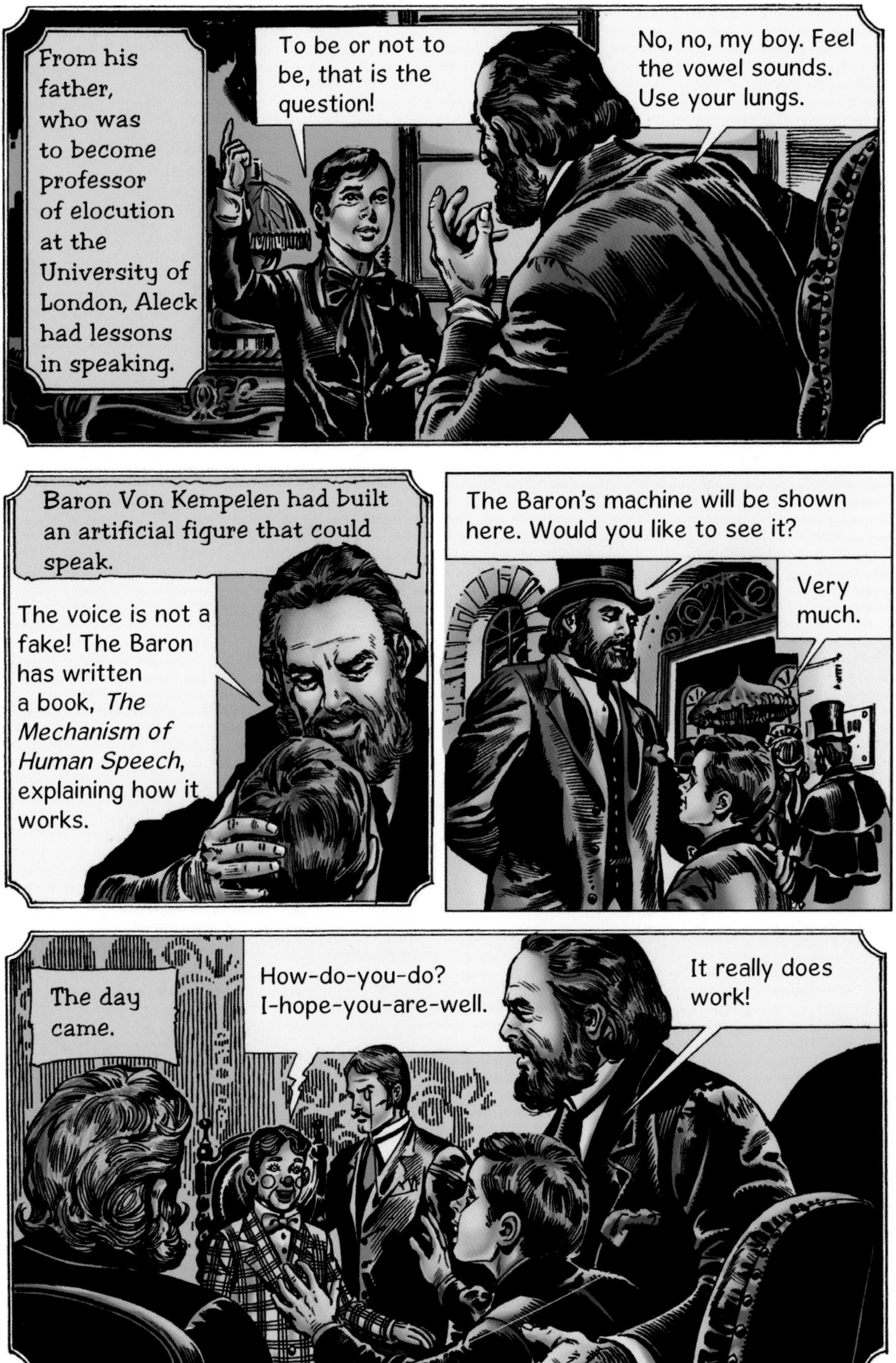
From his father, who was to become professor of elocution at the University of London, Aleck had lessons in speaking.
To be or not to be, that is the question!
No, no, my boy. Feel the vowel sounds. Use your lungs.
Baron Von Kempelen had built an artificial figure that could speak.
The voice is not a fake! The Baron has written a book, *The Mechanism of Human Speech*, explaining how it works.
The Baron's machine will be shown here. Would you like to see it?
Very much.
The day came.
How-do-you-do? I-hope-you-are-well.
It really does work!

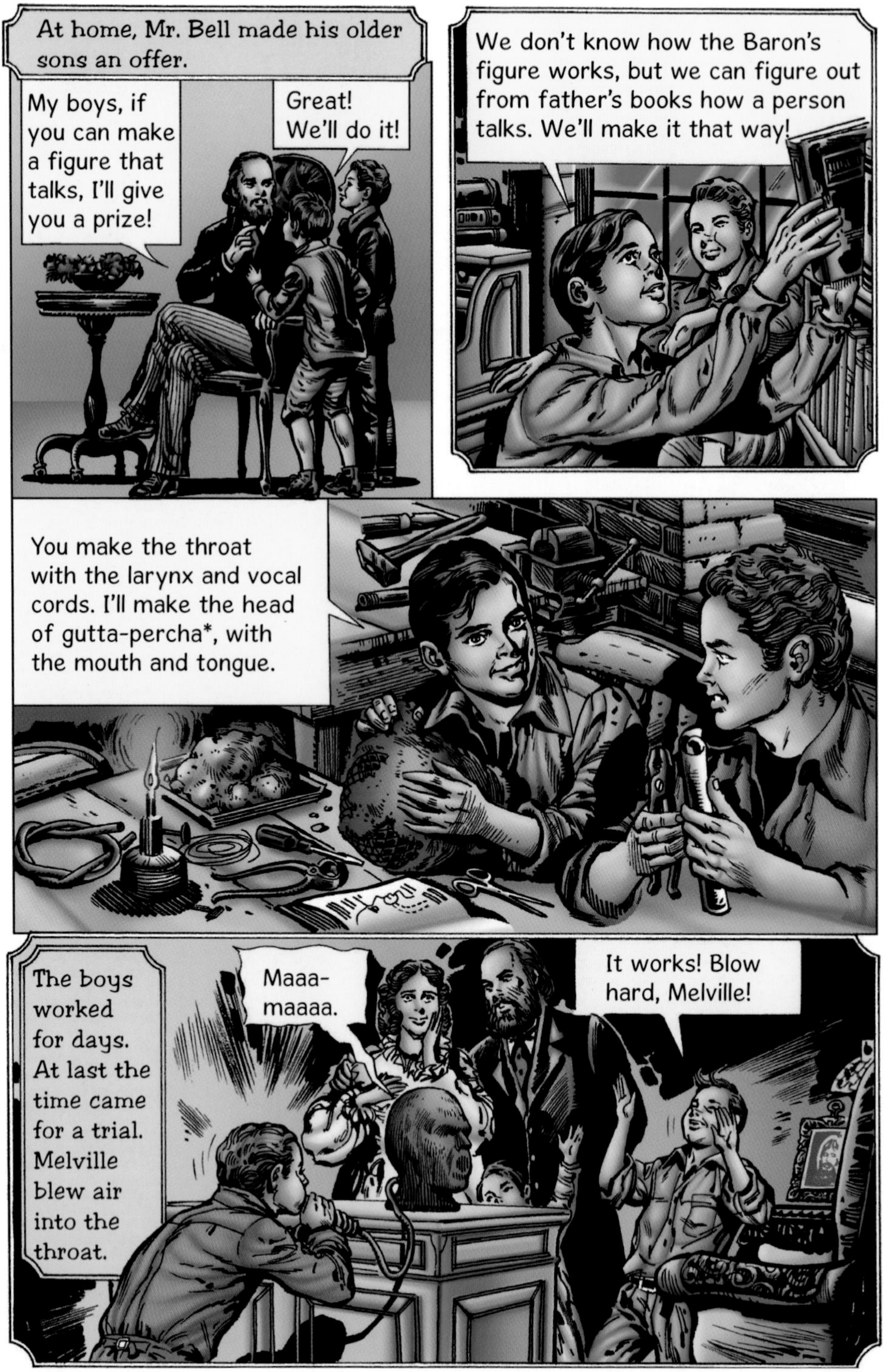
At home, Mr. Bell made his older sons an offer.
My boys, if you can make a figure that talks, I'll give you a prize!
Great! We'll do it!
We don't know how the Baron's figure works, but we can figure out from father's books how a person talks. We'll make it that way!
You make the throat with the larynx and vocal cords. I'll make the head of gutta-percha*, with the mouth and tongue.
The boys worked for days. At last the time came for a trial. Melville blew air into the throat.
Maaa-maaaa.
It works! Blow hard, Melville!

* a tough plastic substance from the latex of several Malaysian trees that resembles rubber

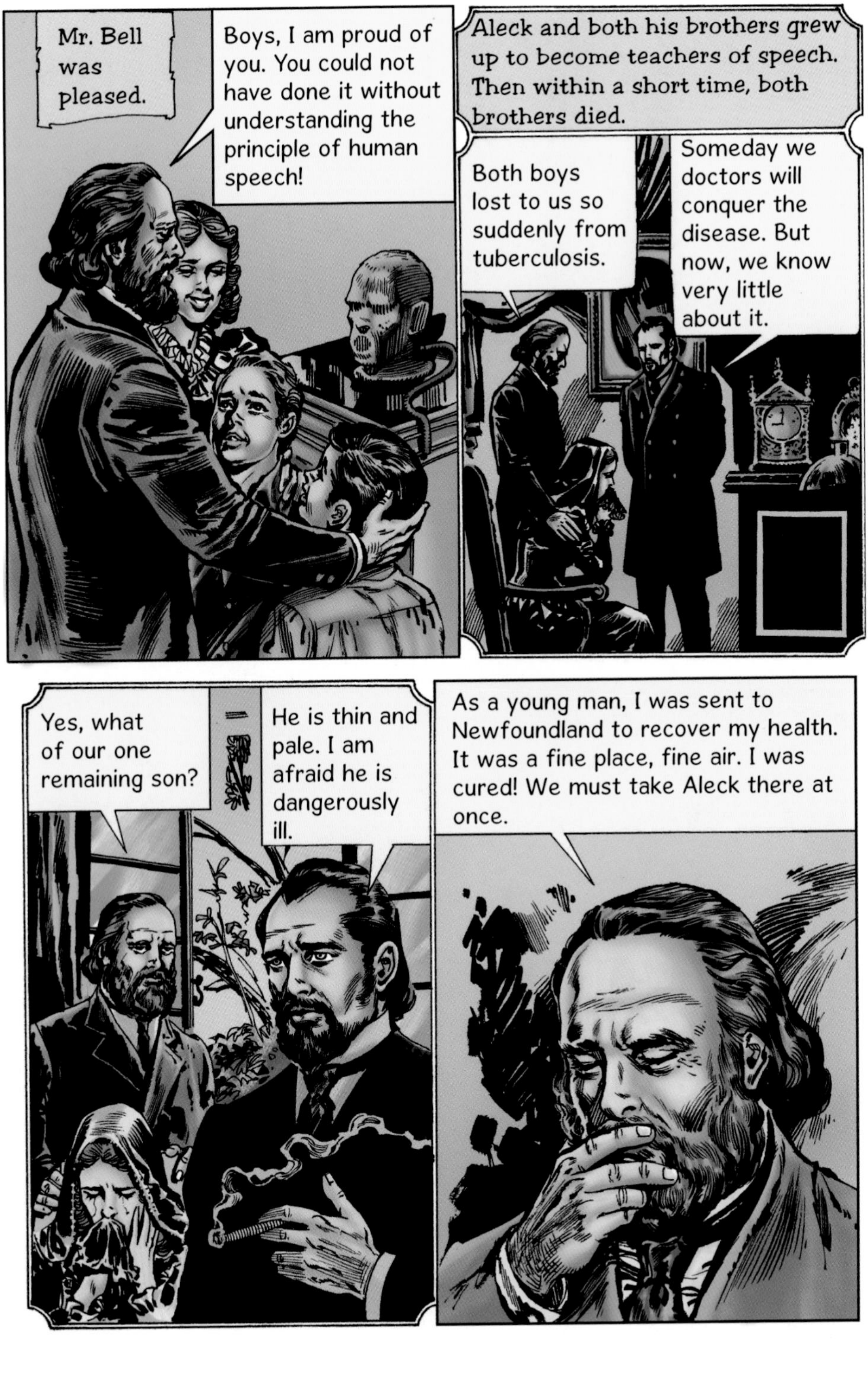
Mr. Bell was pleased.
Boys, I am proud of you. You could not have done it without understanding the principle of human speech!
Aleck and both his brothers grew up to become teachers of speech. Then within a short time, both brothers died.
Both boys lost to us so suddenly from tuberculosis.
Someday we doctors will conquer the disease. But now, we know very little about it.
Yes, what of our one remaining son?
He is thin and pale. I am afraid he is dangerously ill.
As a young man, I was sent to Newfoundland to recover my health. It was a fine place, fine air. I was cured! We must take Aleck there at once.

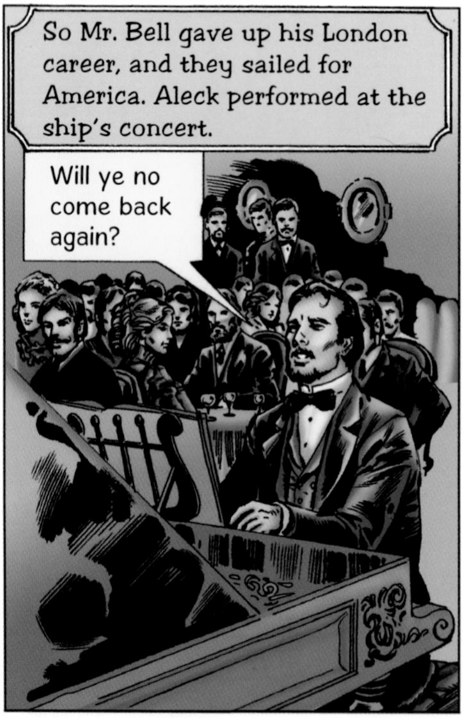
So Mr. Bell gave up his London career, and they sailed for America. Aleck performed at the ship's concert.
Will ye no come back again?

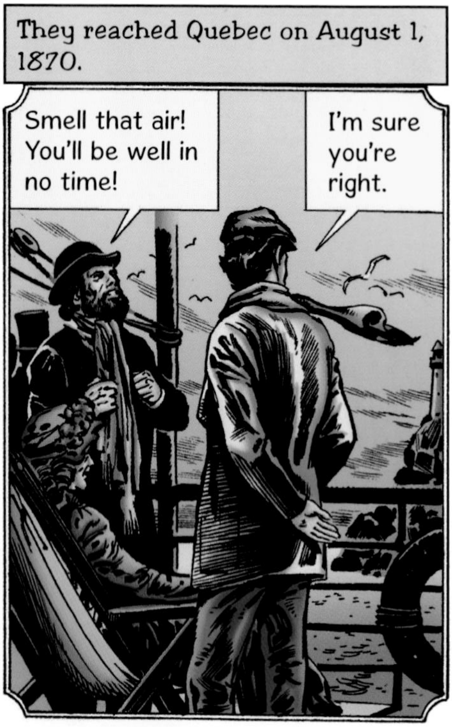
They reached Quebec on August 1, 1870.
Smell that air! You'll be well in no time!
I'm sure you're right.

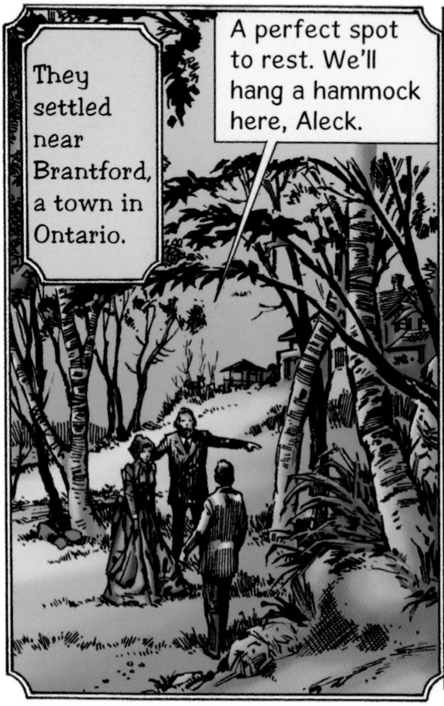
They settled near Brantford, a town in Ontario.
A perfect spot to rest. We'll hang a hammock here, Aleck.

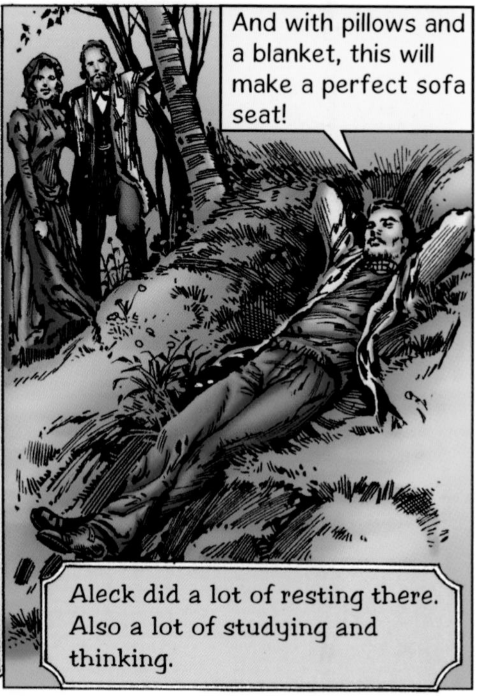
And with pillows and a blanket, this will make a perfect sofa seat!
Aleck did a lot of resting there. Also a lot of studying and thinking.

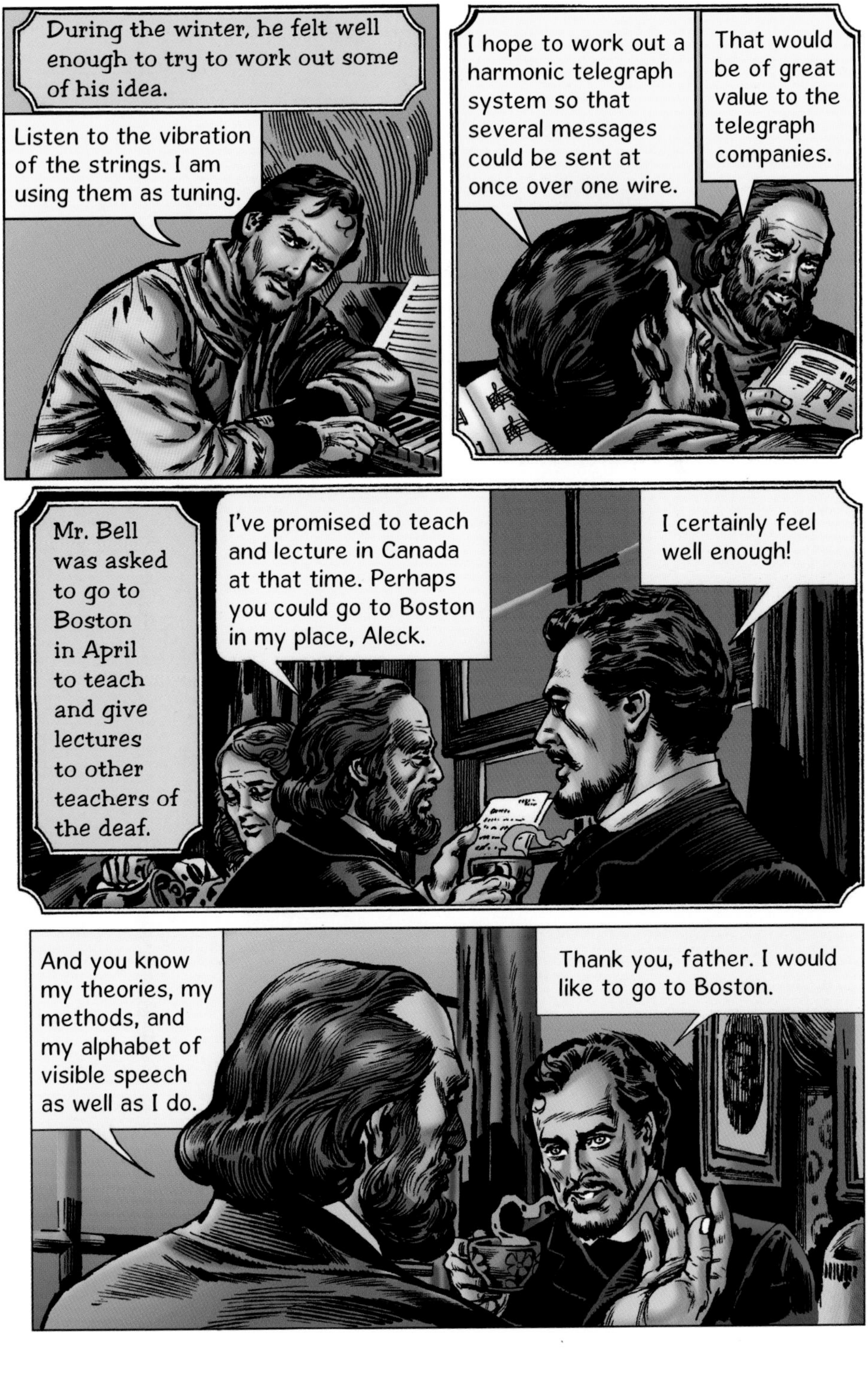
During the winter, he felt well enough to try to work out some of his idea.
Listen to the vibration of the strings. I am using them as tuning.
I hope to work out a harmonic telegraph system so that several messages could be sent at once over one wire.
That would be of great value to the telegraph companies.
Mr. Bell was asked to go to Boston in April to teach and give lectures to other teachers of the deaf.
I've promised to teach and lecture in Canada at that time. Perhaps you could go to Boston in my place, Aleck.
I certainly feel well enough!
And you know my theories, my methods, and my alphabet of visible speech as well as I do.
Thank you, father. I would like to go to Boston.

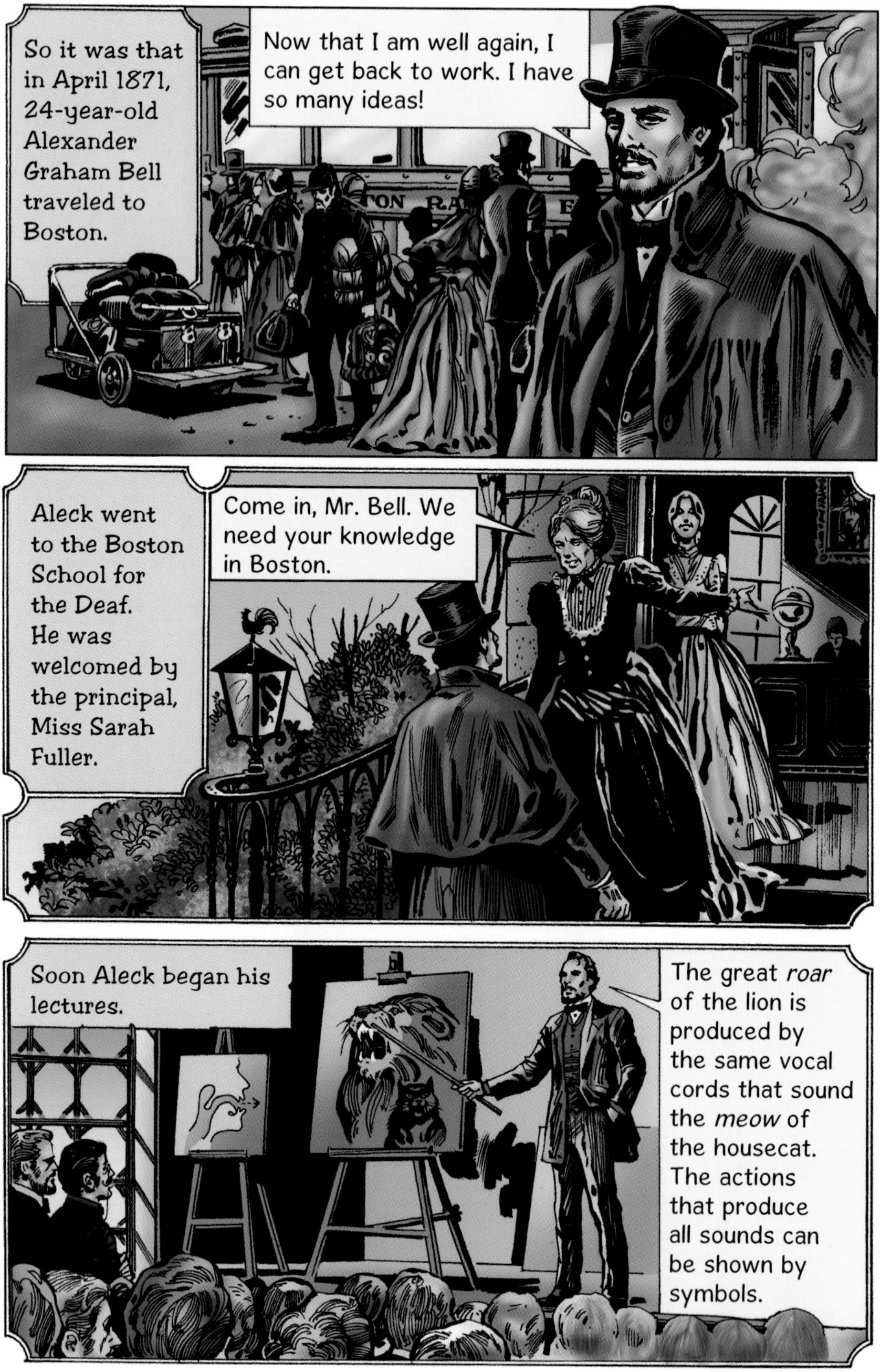
So it was that in April 1871, 24-year-old Alexander Graham Bell traveled to Boston.
Now that I am well again, I can get back to work. I have so many ideas!
TON RA
E
Aleck went to the Boston School for the Deaf. He was welcomed by the principal, Miss Sarah Fuller.
Come in, Mr. Bell. We need your knowledge in Boston.
Soon Aleck began his lectures.
The great *roar* of the lion is produced by the same vocal cords that sound the *meow* of the housecat. The actions that produce all sounds can be shown by symbols.

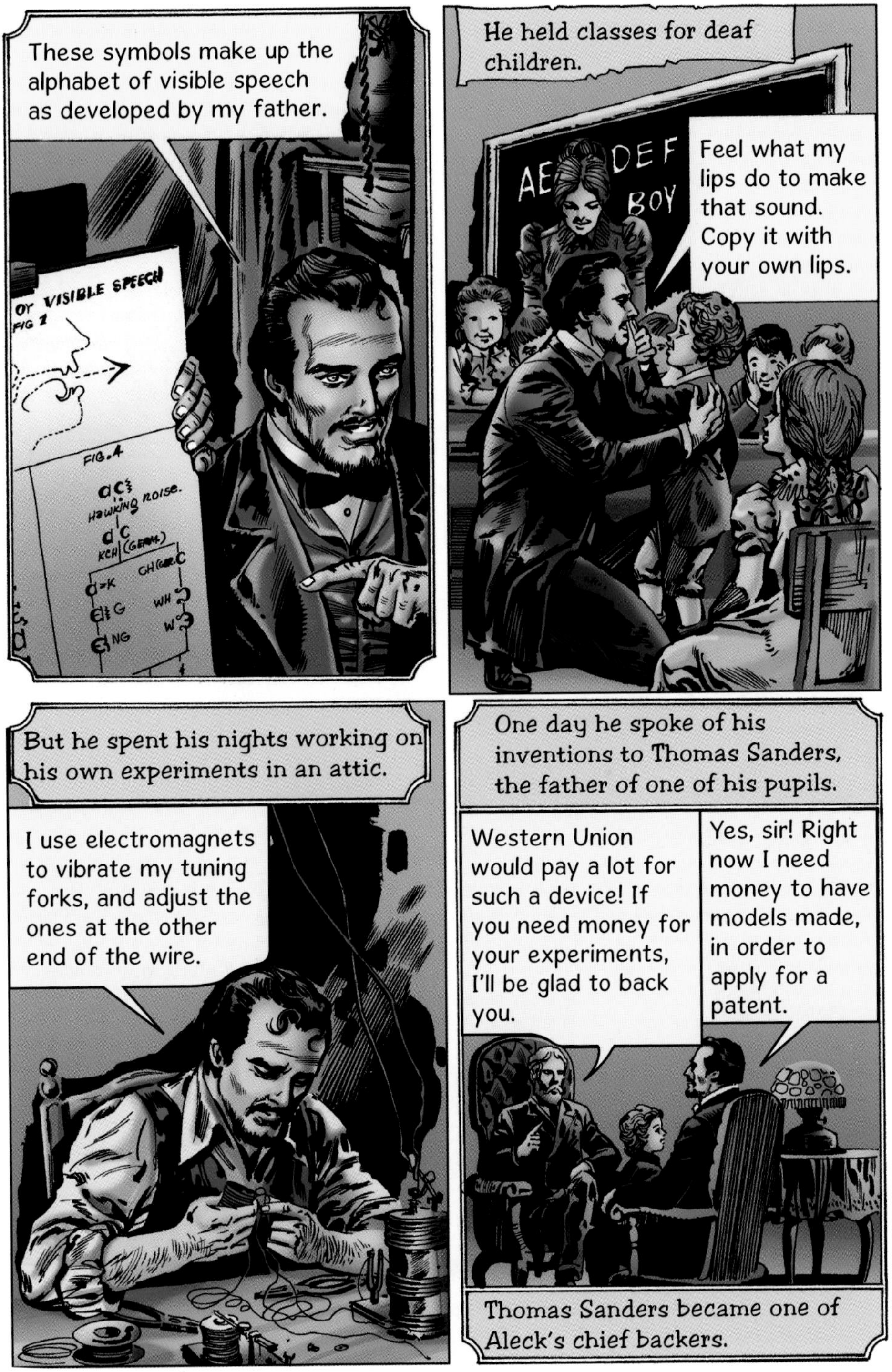
These symbols make up the alphabet of visible speech as developed by my father.
VISIBLE SPEECH
He held classes for deaf children.
BOY
Feel what my lips do to make that sound. Copy it with your own lips.
But he spent his nights working on his own experiments in an attic.
I use electromagnets to vibrate my tuning forks, and adjust the ones at the other end of the wire.
One day he spoke of his inventions to Thomas Sanders, the father of one of his pupils.
Western Union would pay a lot for such a device! If you need money for your experiments, I'll be glad to back you.
Yes, sir! Right now I need money to have models made, in order to apply for a patent.
Thomas Sanders became one of Aleck's chief backers.

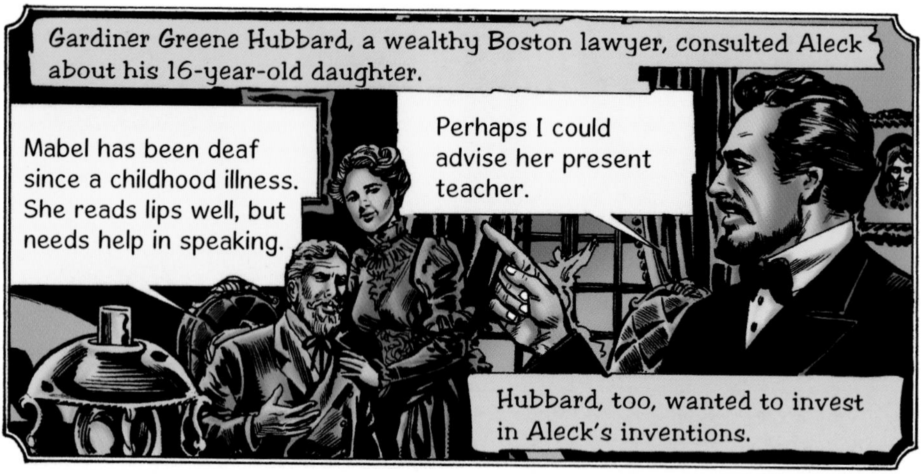
Gardiner Greene Hubbard, a wealthy Boston lawyer, consulted Aleck about his 16-year-old daughter.
Mabel has been deaf since a childhood illness. She reads lips well, but needs help in speaking.
Perhaps I could advise her present teacher.
Hubbard, too, wanted to invest in Aleck's inventions.

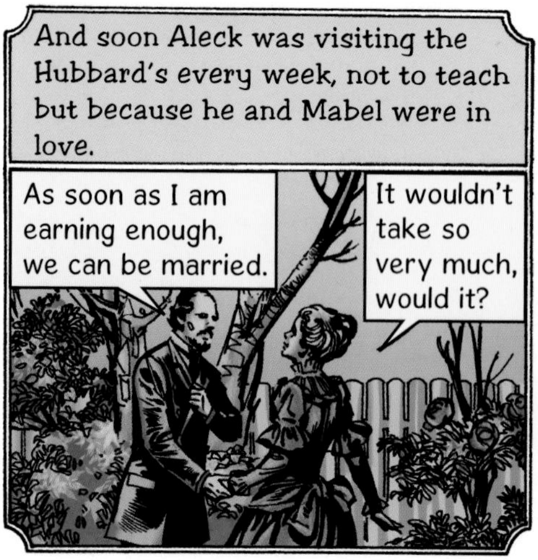
And soon Aleck was visiting the Hubbard's every week, not to teach but because he and Mabel were in love.
As soon as I am earning enough, we can be married.
It wouldn't take so very much, would it?

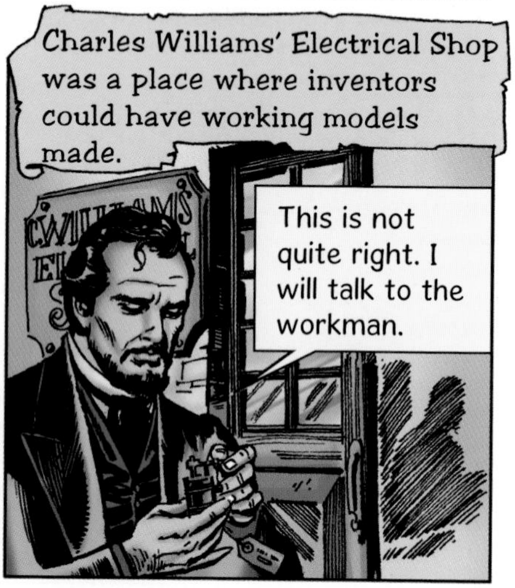
Charles Williams' Electrical Shop was a place where inventors could have working models made.
This is not quite right. I will talk to the workman.

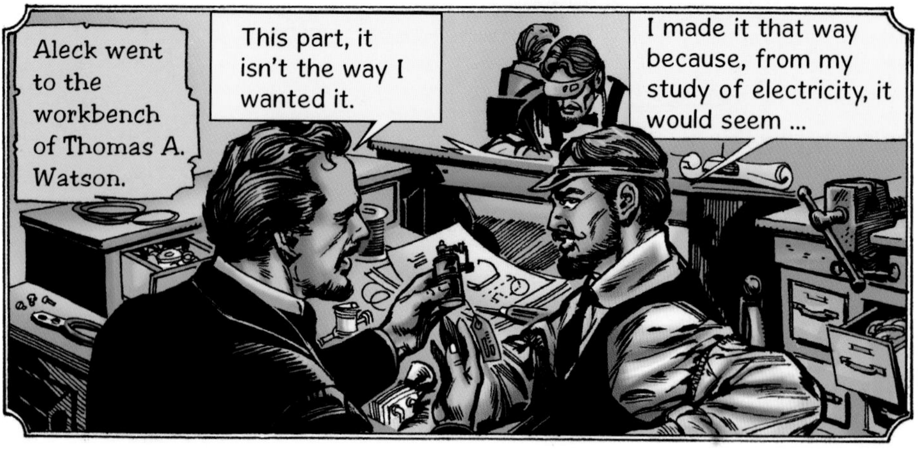
Aleck went to the workbench of Thomas A. Watson.
This part, it isn't the way I wanted it.
I made it that way because, from my study of electricity, it would seem ...

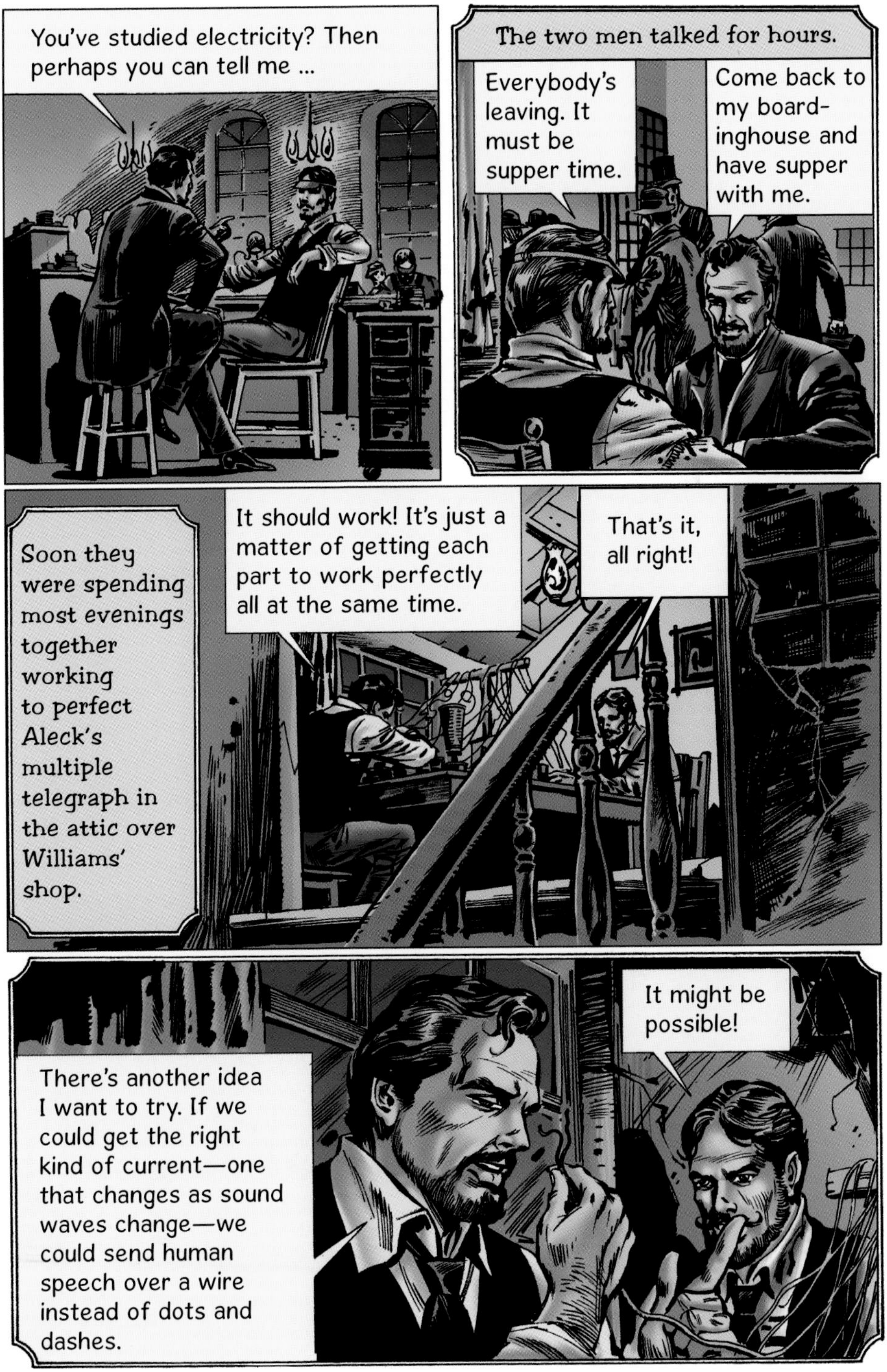
You've studied electricity? Then perhaps you can tell me ...
The two men talked for hours.
Everybody's leaving. It must be supper time.
Come back to my board-inghouse and have supper with me.
Soon they were spending most evenings together working to perfect Aleck's multiple telegraph in the attic over Williams' shop.
It should work! It's just a matter of getting each part to work perfectly all at the same time.
That's it, all right!
There's another idea I want to try. If we could get the right kind of current—one that changes as sound waves change—we could send human speech over a wire instead of dots and dashes.
It might be possible!

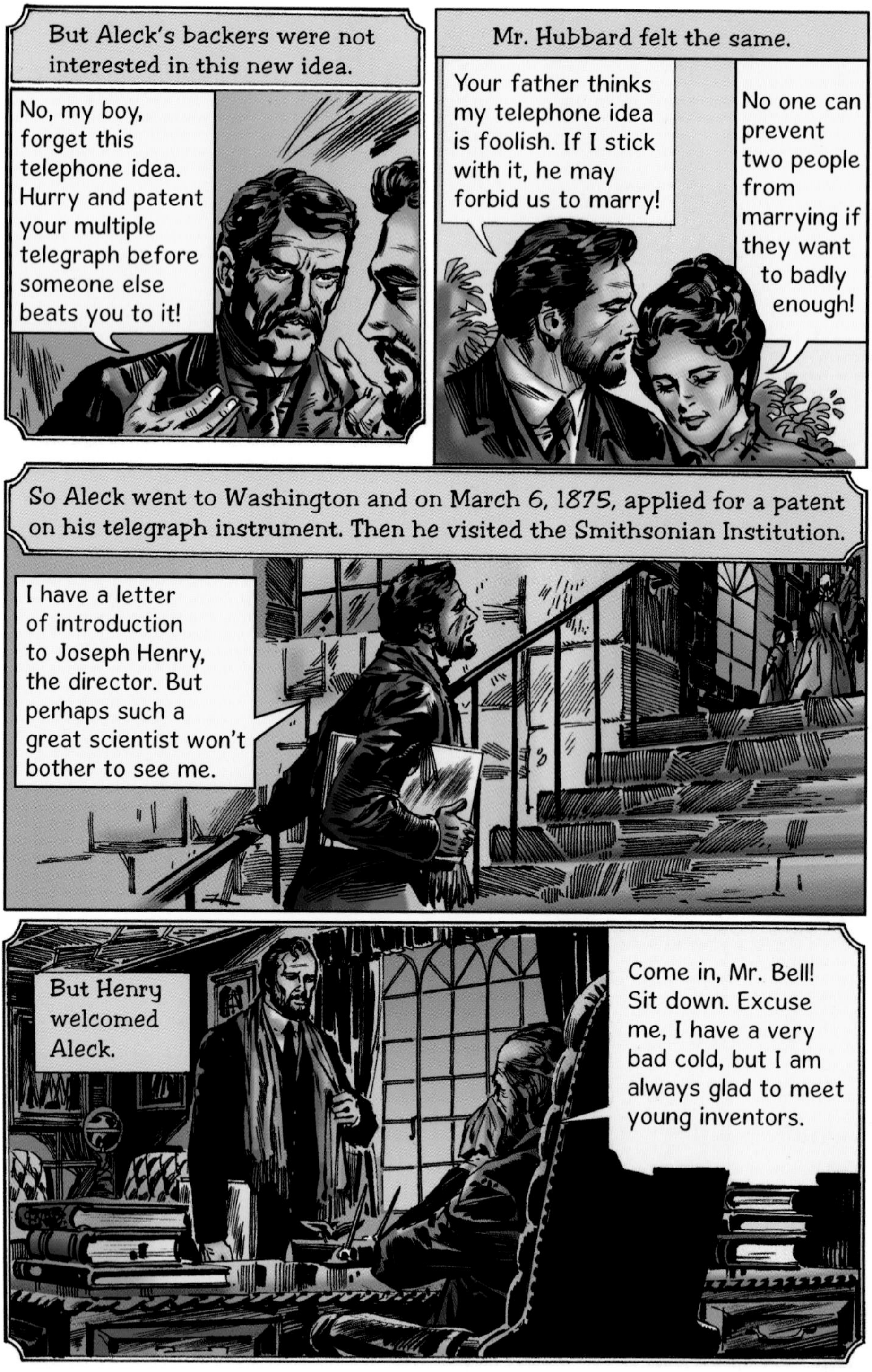
But Aleck's backers were not interested in this new idea.
No, my boy, forget this telephone idea. Hurry and patent your multiple telegraph before someone else beats you to it!
Mr. Hubbard felt the same.
Your father thinks my telephone idea is foolish. If I stick with it, he may forbid us to marry!
No one can prevent two people from marrying if they want to badly enough!
So Aleck went to Washington and on March 6, 1875, applied for a patent on his telegraph instrument. Then he visited the Smithsonian Institution.
I have a letter of introduction to Joseph Henry, the director. But perhaps such a great scientist won't bother to see me.
But Henry welcomed Aleck.
Come in, Mr. Bell! Sit down. Excuse me, I have a very bad cold, but I am always glad to meet young inventors.

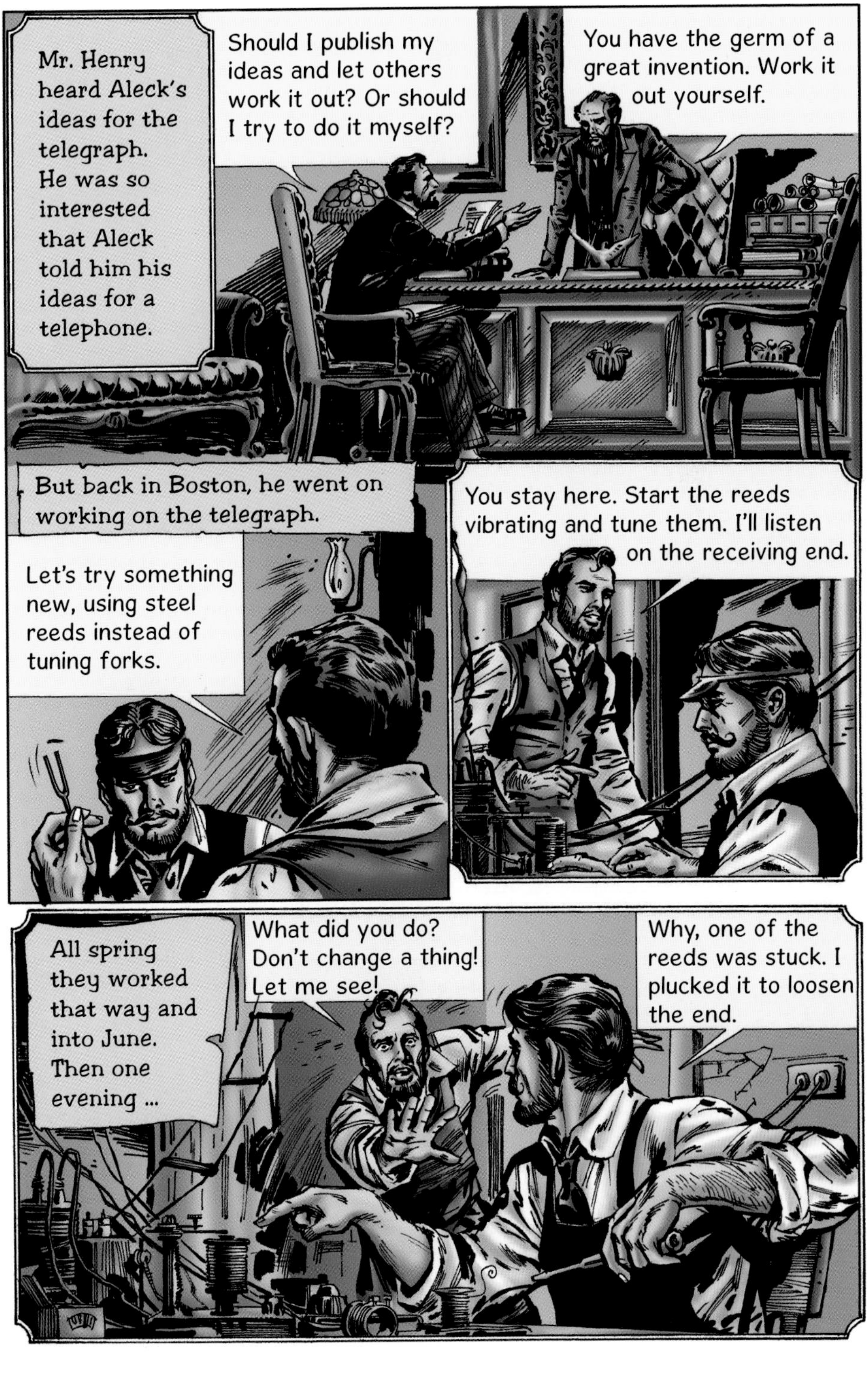
Mr. Henry heard Aleck's ideas for the telegraph. He was so interested that Aleck told him his ideas for a telephone.
Should I publish my ideas and let others work it out? Or should I try to do it myself?
You have the germ of a great invention. Work it out yourself.
But back in Boston, he went on working on the telegraph.
Let's try something new, using steel reeds instead of tuning forks.
You stay here. Start the reeds vibrating and tune them. I'll listen on the receiving end.
All spring they worked that way and into June. Then one evening ...
What did you do? Don't change a thing! Let me see!
Why, one of the reeds was stuck. I plucked it to loosen the end.

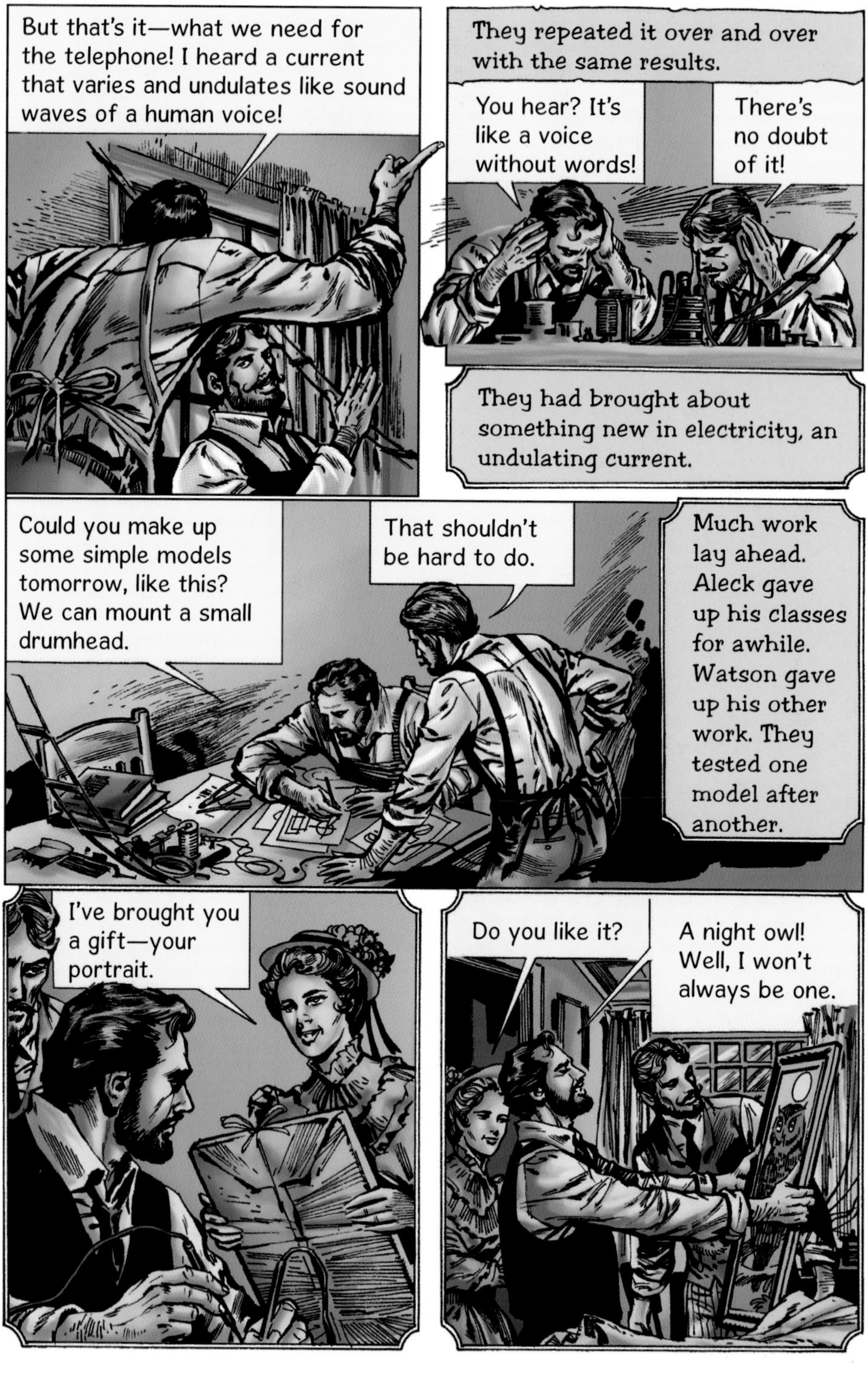

But that's it—what we need for the telephone! I heard a current that varies and undulates like sound waves of a human voice!
They repeated it over and over with the same results.
You hear? It's like a voice without words!
There's no doubt of it!
They had brought about something new in electricity, an undulating current.
Could you make up some simple models tomorrow, like this? We can mount a small drumhead.
That shouldn't be hard to do.
Much work lay ahead. Aleck gave up his classes for awhile. Watson gave up his other work. They tested one model after another.
I've brought you a gift—your portrait.
Do you like it?
A night owl! Well, I won't always be one.

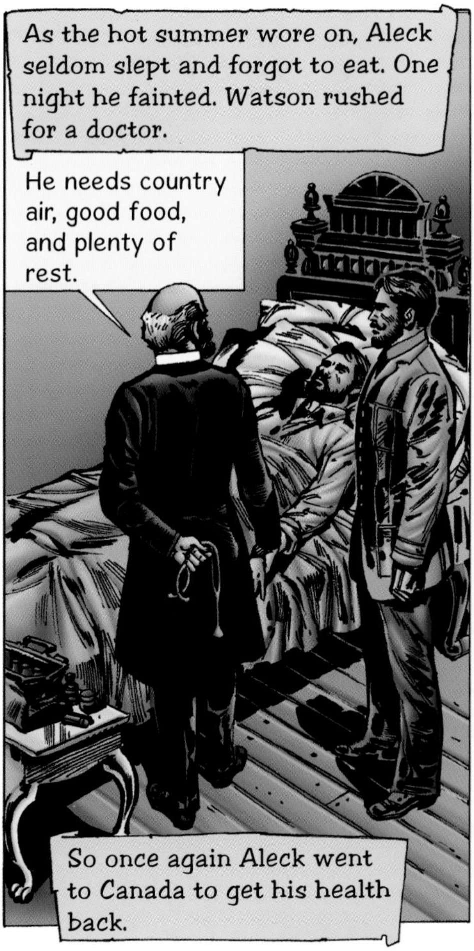
As the hot summer wore on, Aleck seldom slept and forgot to eat. One night he fainted. Watson rushed for a doctor.
He needs country air, good food, and plenty of rest.
So once again Aleck went to Canada to get his health back.

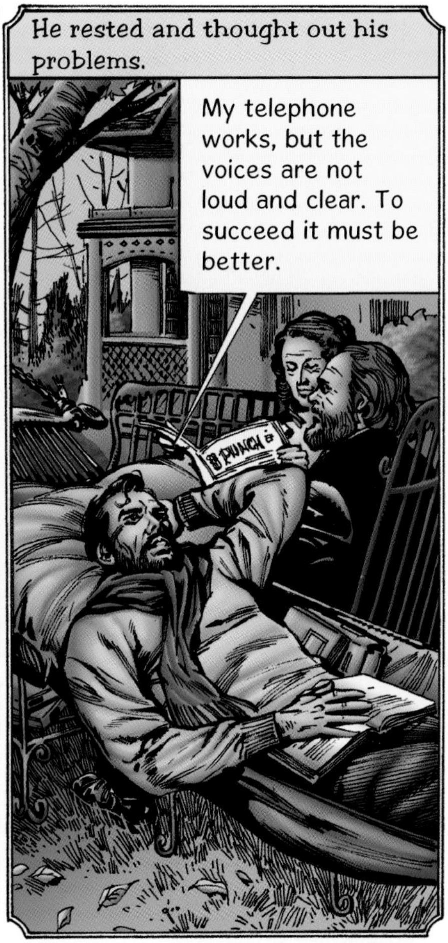
He rested and thought out his problems.
My telephone works, but the voices are not loud and clear. To succeed it must be better.
PUNCH

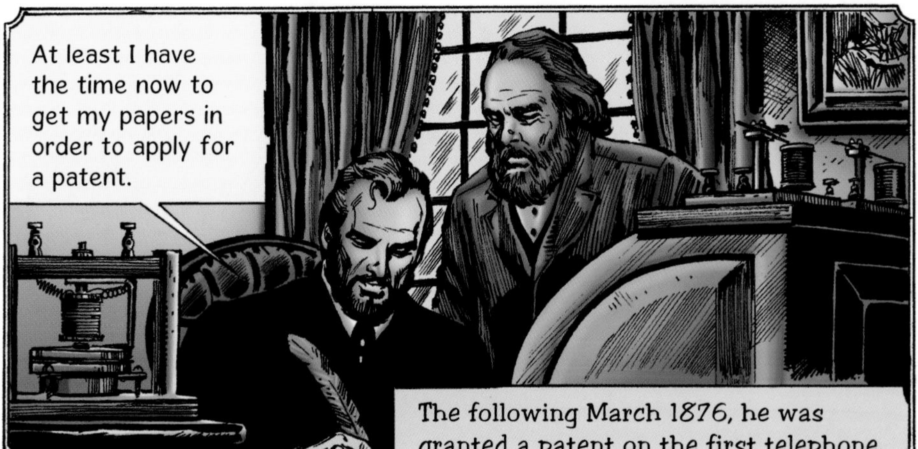
At least I have the time now to get my papers in order to apply for a patent.
The following March 1876, he was granted a patent on the first telephone.

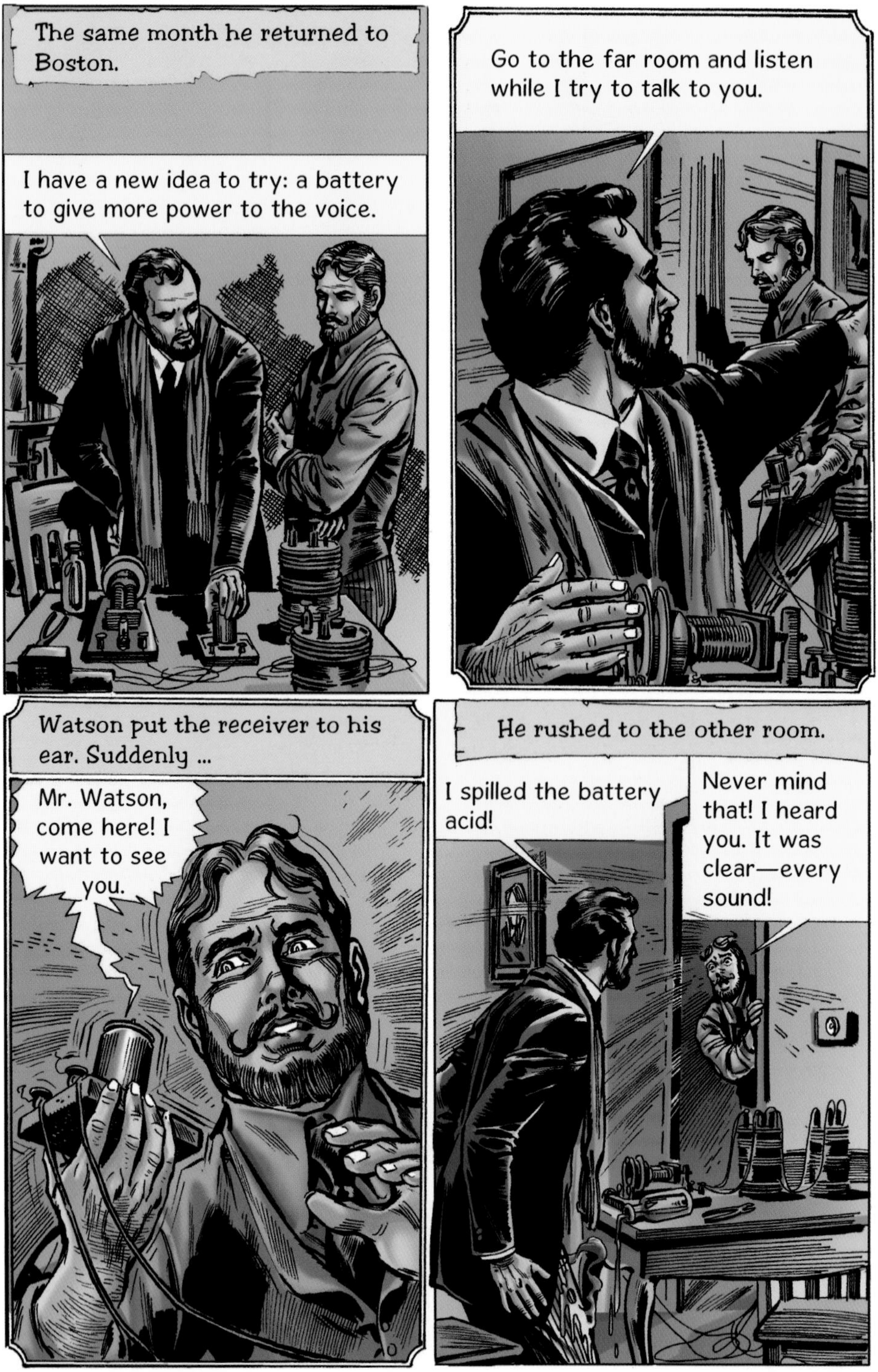
The same month he returned to Boston.
I have a new idea to try: a battery to give more power to the voice.
Go to the far room and listen while I try to talk to you.
Watson put the receiver to his ear. Suddenly ...
Mr. Watson, come here! I want to see you.
He rushed to the other room.
I spilled the battery acid!
Never mind that! I heard you. It was clear—every sound!

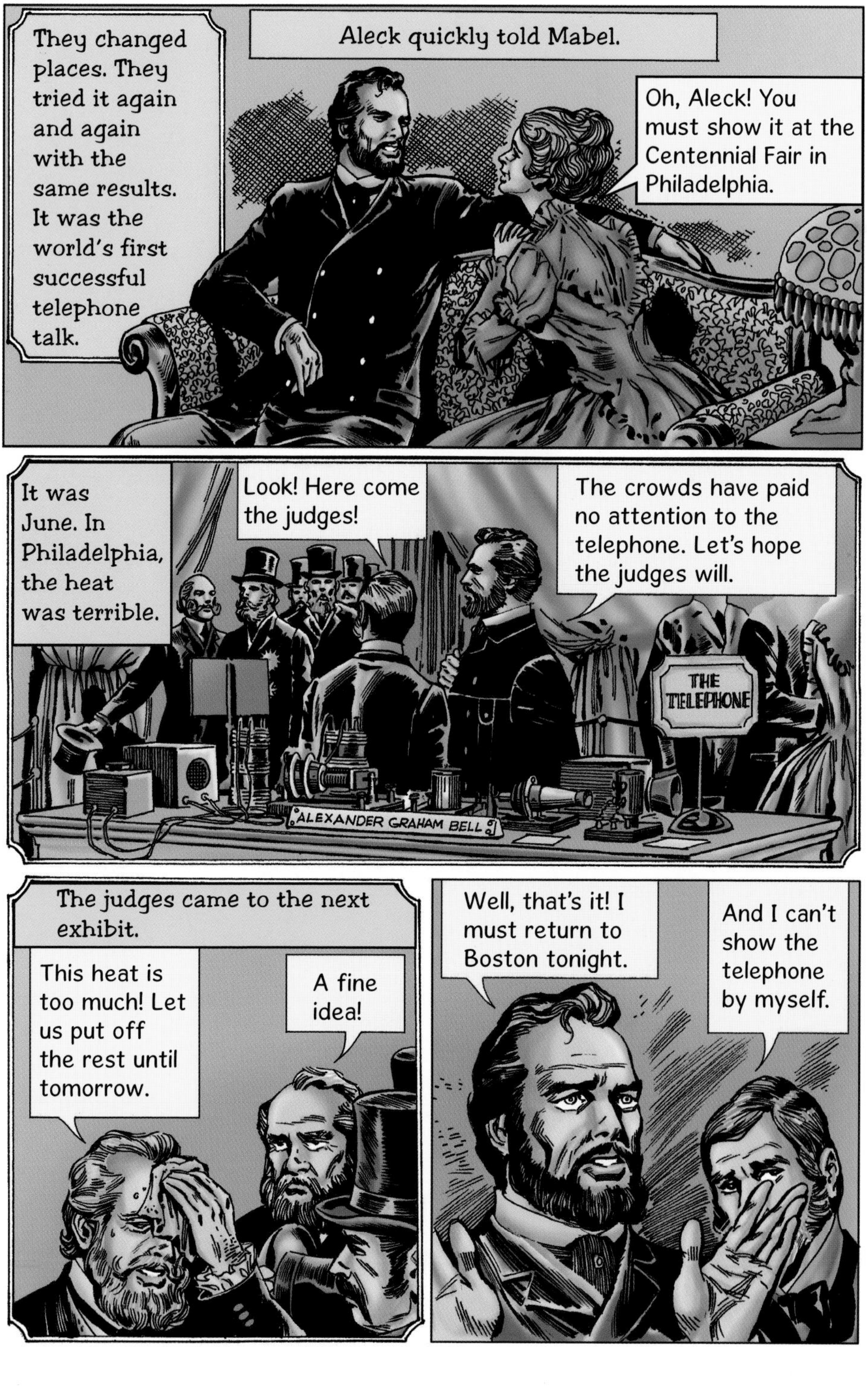
They changed places. They tried it again and again with the same results. It was the world's first successful telephone talk.
Aleck quickly told Mabel.
Oh, Aleck! You must show it at the Centennial Fair in Philadelphia.
It was June. In Philadelphia, the heat was terrible.
Look! Here come the judges!
The crowds have paid no attention to the telephone. Let's hope the judges will.
THE TELEPHONE
ALEXANDER GRAHAM BELL
The judges came to the next exhibit.
This heat is too much! Let us put off the rest until tomorrow.
A fine idea!
Well, that's it! I must return to Boston tonight.
And I can't show the telephone by myself.

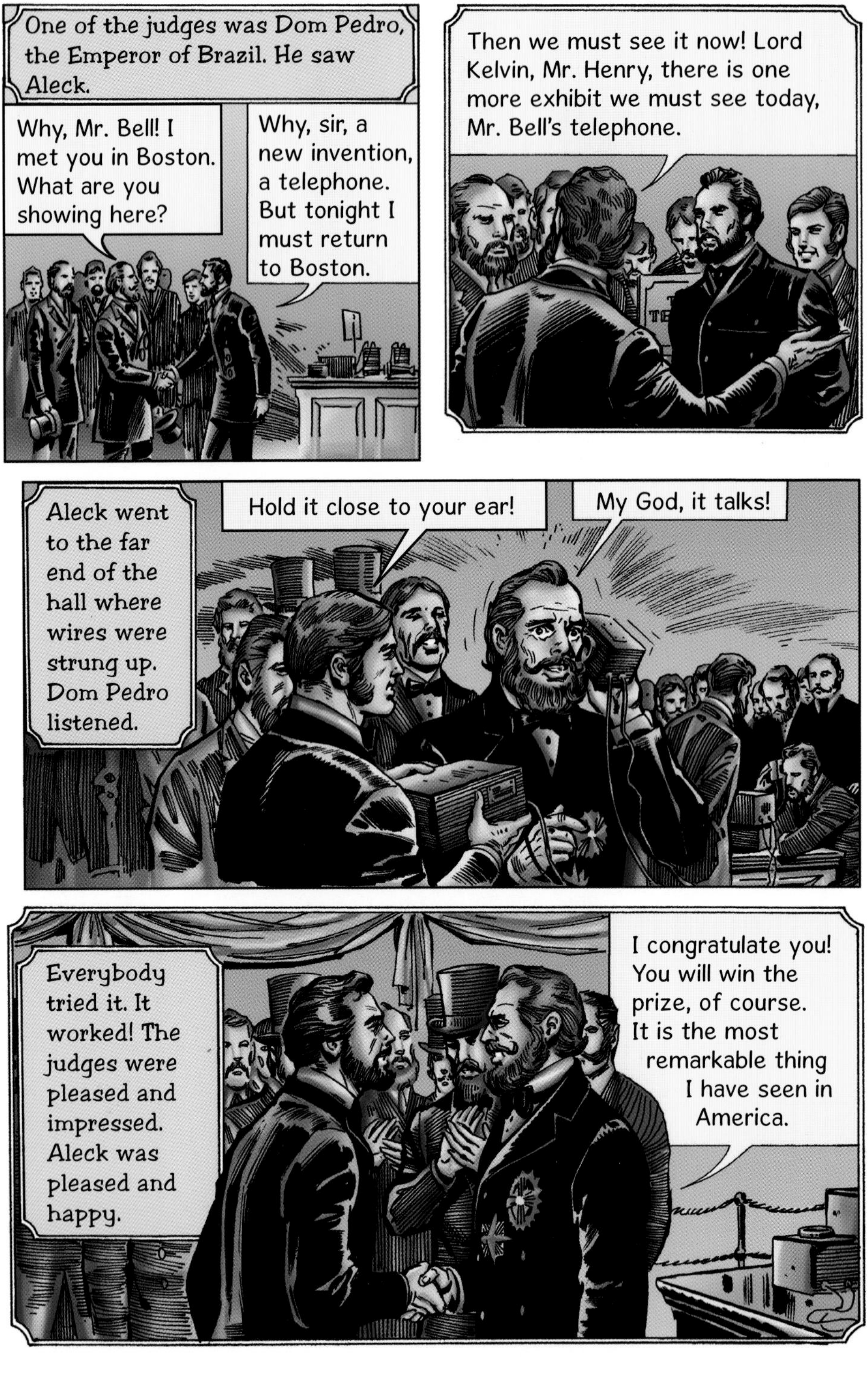
One of the judges was Dom Pedro, the Emperor of Brazil. He saw Aleck.
Why, Mr. Bell! I met you in Boston. What are you showing here?
Why, sir, a new invention, a telephone. But tonight I must return to Boston.
Then we must see it now! Lord Kelvin, Mr. Henry, there is one more exhibit we must see today, Mr. Bell's telephone.
Aleck went to the far end of the hall where wires were strung up. Dom Pedro listened.
Hold it close to your ear!
My God, it talks!
Everybody tried it. It worked! The judges were pleased and impressed. Aleck was pleased and happy.
I congratulate you! You will win the prize, of course. It is the most remarkable thing I have seen in America.

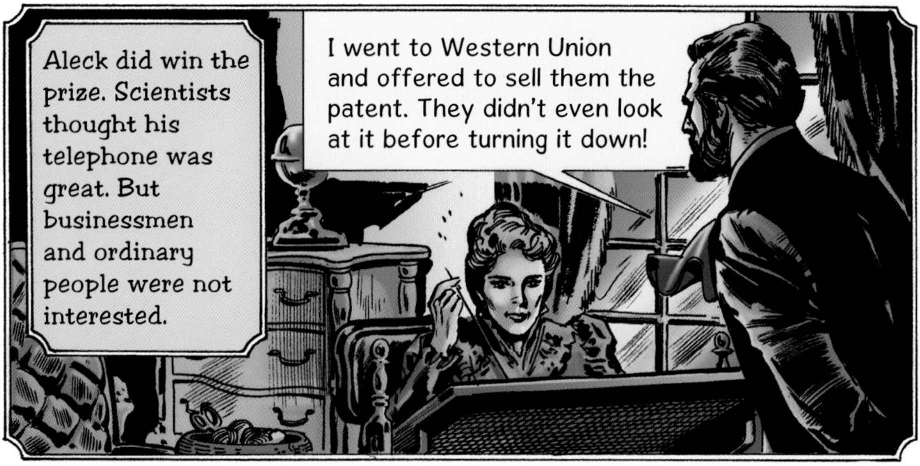
Aleck did win the prize. Scientists thought his telephone was great. But businessmen and ordinary people were not interested.
I went to Western Union and offered to sell them the patent. They didn't even look at it before turning it down!

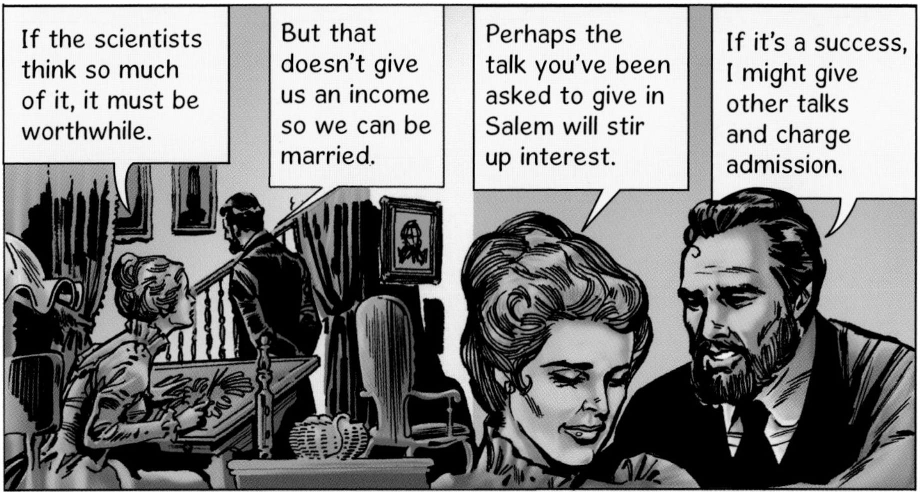
If the scientists think so much of it, it must be worthwhile.
But that doesn't give us an income so we can be married.
Perhaps the talk you've been asked to give in Salem will stir up interest.
If it's a success, I might give other talks and charge admission.

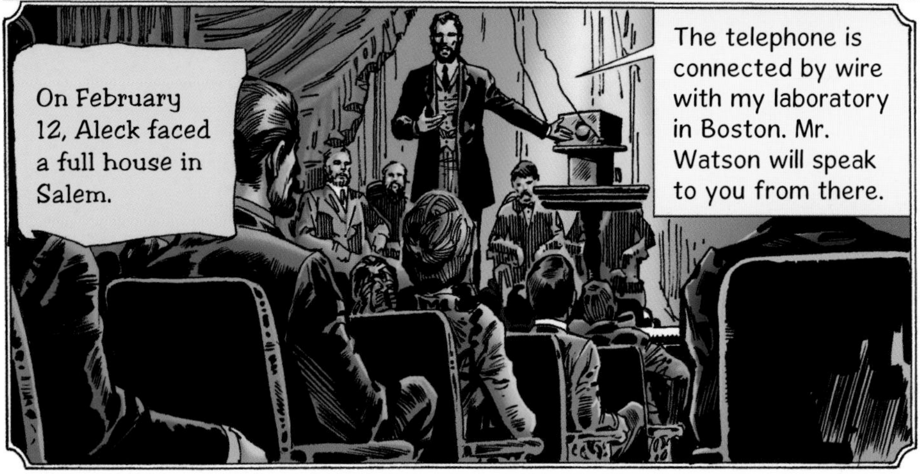
On February 12, Aleck faced a full house in Salem.
The telephone is connected by wire with my laboratory in Boston. Mr. Watson will speak to you from there.

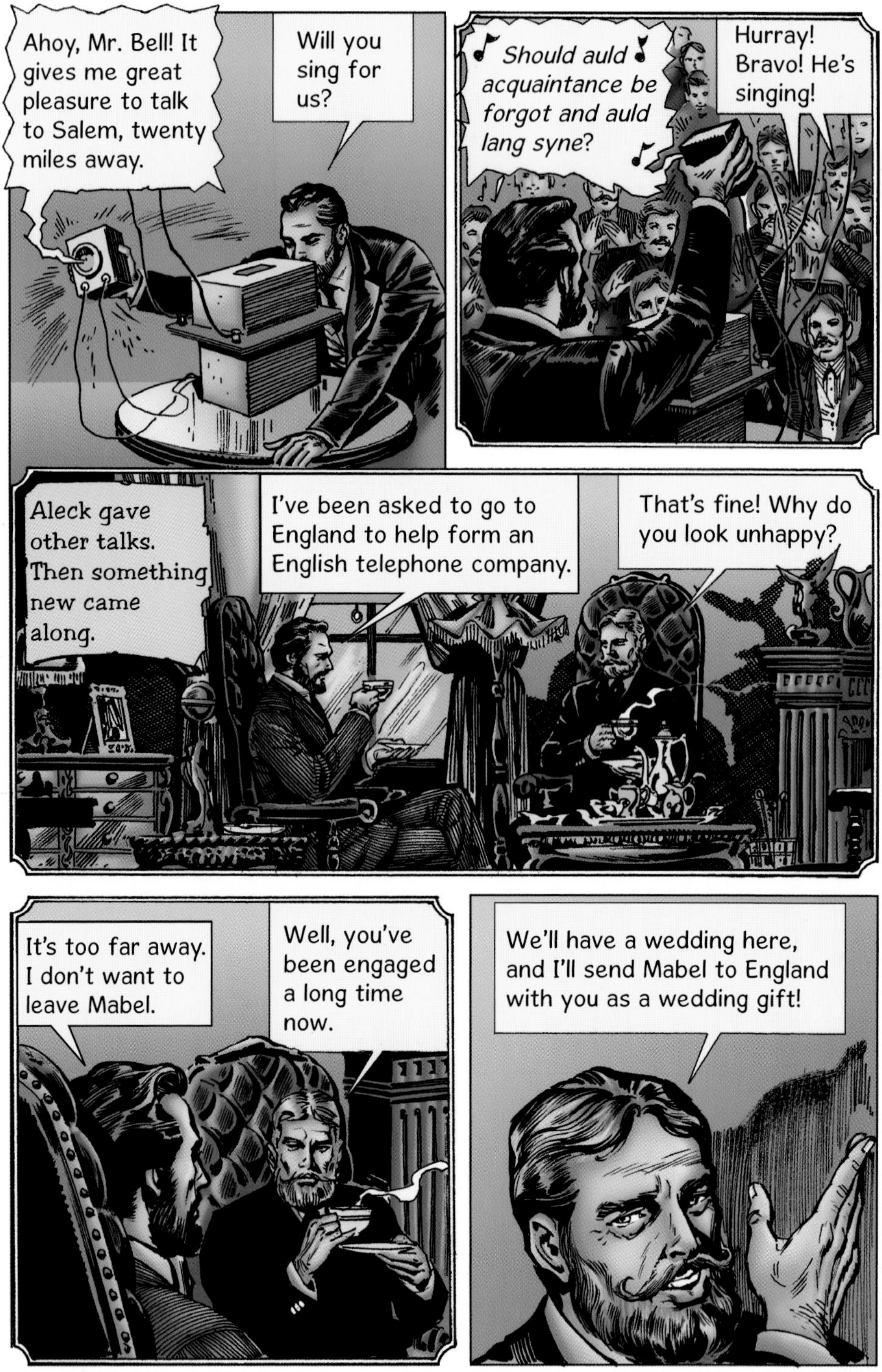
Ahoy, Mr. Bell! It gives me great pleasure to talk to Salem, twenty miles away.
Will you sing for us?
Should auld acquaintance be forgot and auld lang syne?
Hurray! Bravo! He's singing!
Aleck gave other talks. Then something new came along.
I've been asked to go to England to help form an English telephone company.
That's fine! Why do you look unhappy?
It's too far away. I don't want to leave Mabel.
Well, you've been engaged a long time now.
We'll have a wedding here, and I'll send Mabel to England with you as a wedding gift!

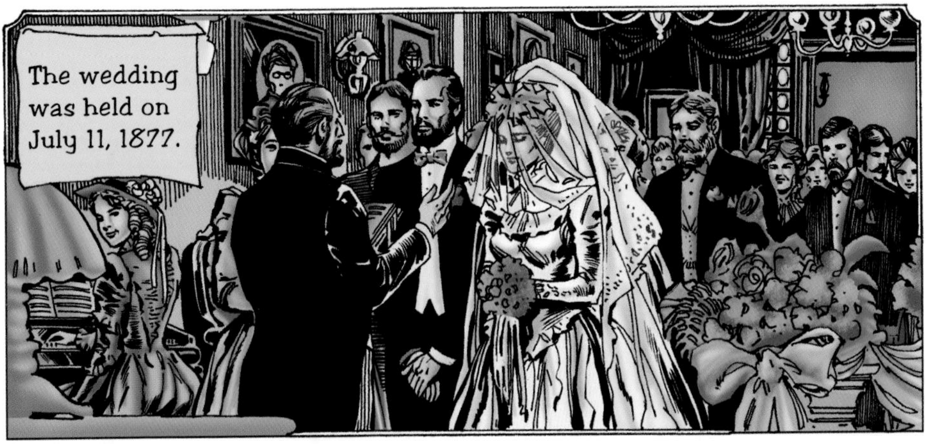
The wedding was held on July 11, 1877.

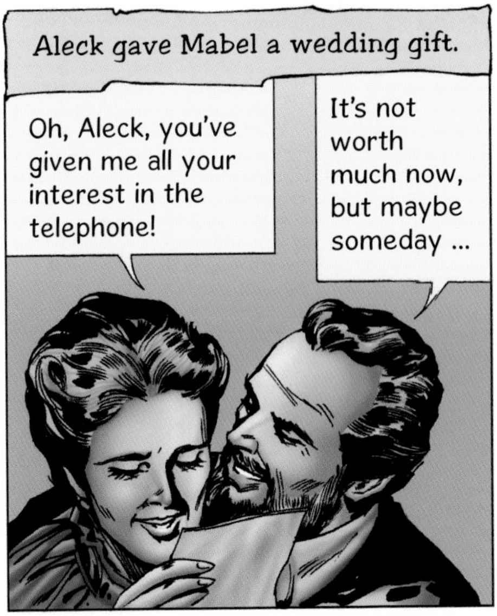
Aleck gave Mabel a wedding gift.
Oh, Aleck, you've given me all your interest in the telephone!
It's not worth much now, but maybe someday ...

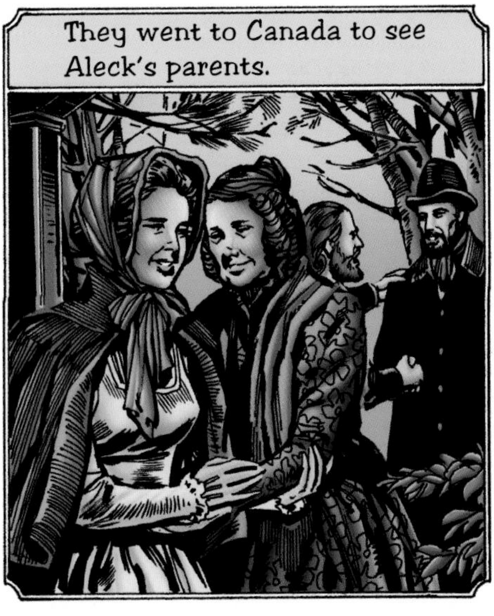
They went to Canada to see Aleck's parents.

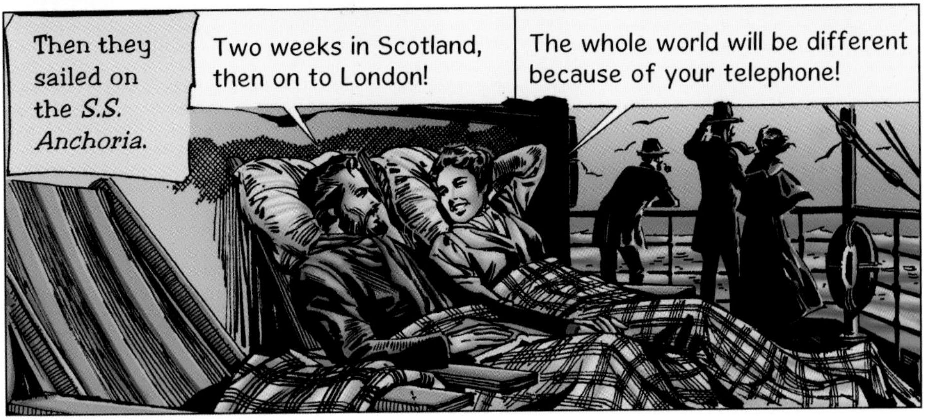
Then they sailed on the *S.S. Anchoria.*
Two weeks in Scotland, then on to London!
The whole world will be different because of your telephone!

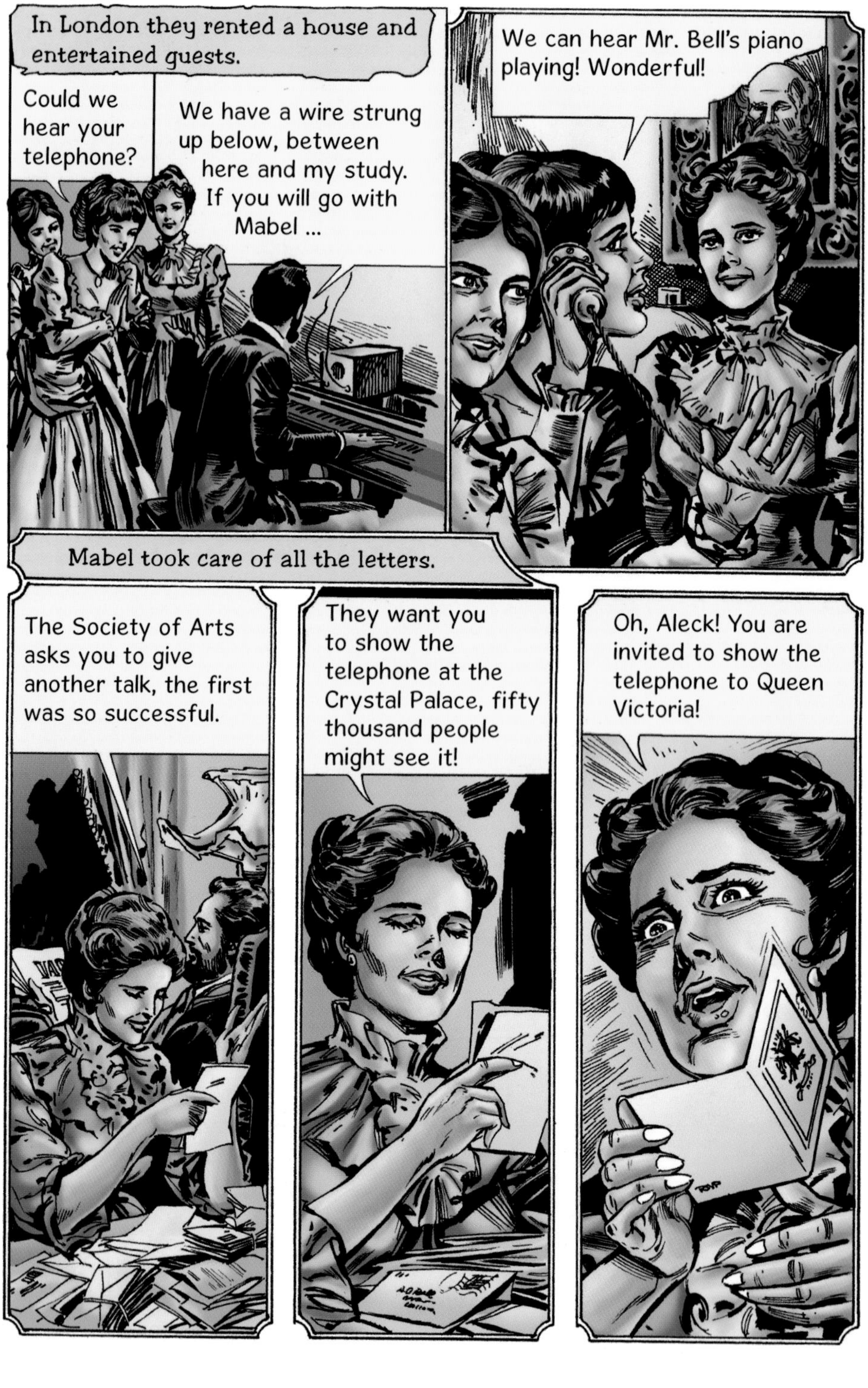
In London they rented a house and entertained guests.
Could we hear your telephone?
We have a wire strung up below, between here and my study. If you will go with Mabel ...
We can hear Mr. Bell's piano playing! Wonderful!
Mabel took care of all the letters.
The Society of Arts asks you to give another talk, the first was so successful.
They want you to show the telephone at the Crystal Palace, fifty thousand people might see it!
Oh, Aleck! You are invited to show the telephone to Queen Victoria!

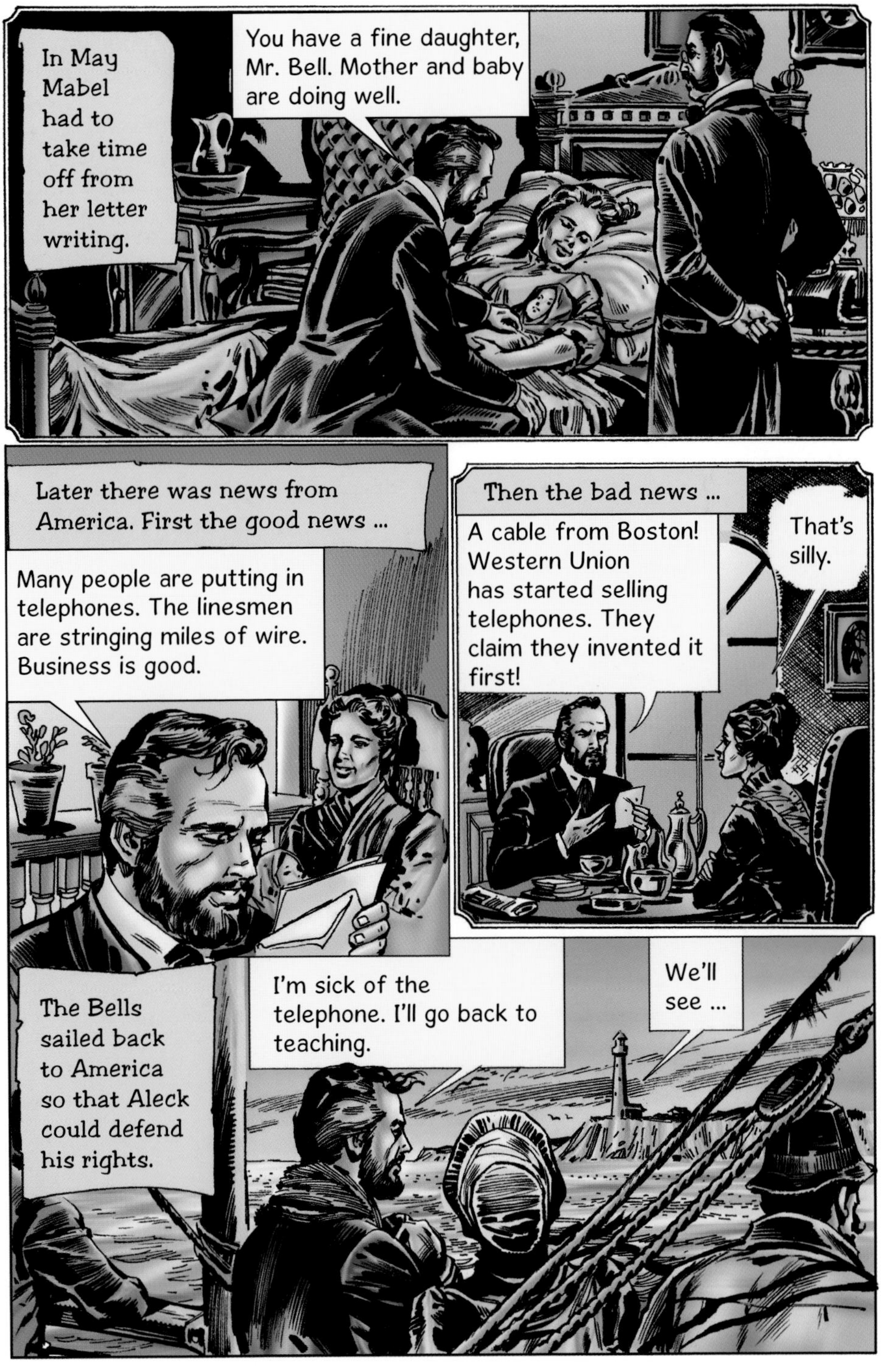
In May Mabel had to take time off from her letter writing.
You have a fine daughter, Mr. Bell. Mother and baby are doing well.
Later there was news from America. First the good news ...
Many people are putting in telephones. The linesmen are stringing miles of wire. Business is good.
Then the bad news ...
A cable from Boston! Western Union has started selling telephones. They claim they invented it first!
That's silly.
The Bells sailed back to America so that Aleck could defend his rights.
I'm sick of the telephone. I'll go back to teaching.
We'll see ...

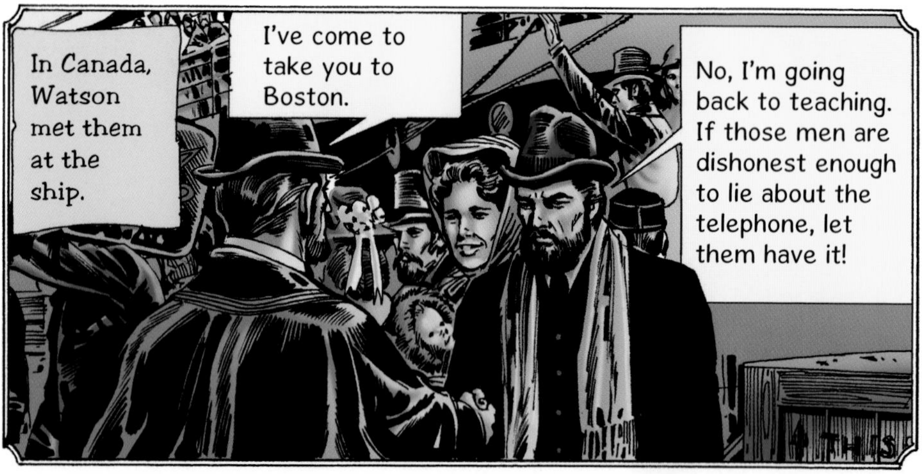
In Canada, Watson met them at the ship.
I've come to take you to Boston.
No, I'm going back to teaching. If those men are dishonest enough to lie about the telephone, let them have it!

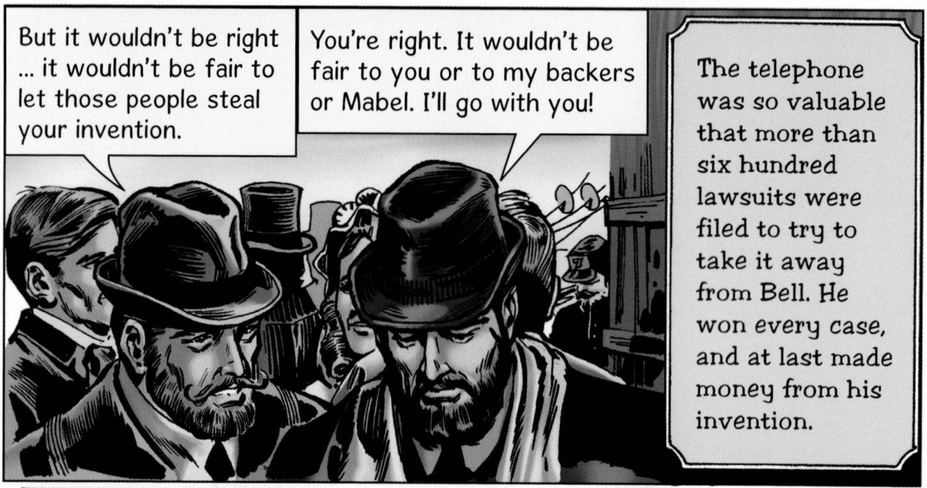
But it wouldn't be right ... it wouldn't be fair to let those people steal your invention.
You're right. It wouldn't be fair to you or to my backers or Mabel. I'll go with you!
The telephone was so valuable that more than six hundred lawsuits were filed to try to take it away from Bell. He won every case, and at last made money from his invention.

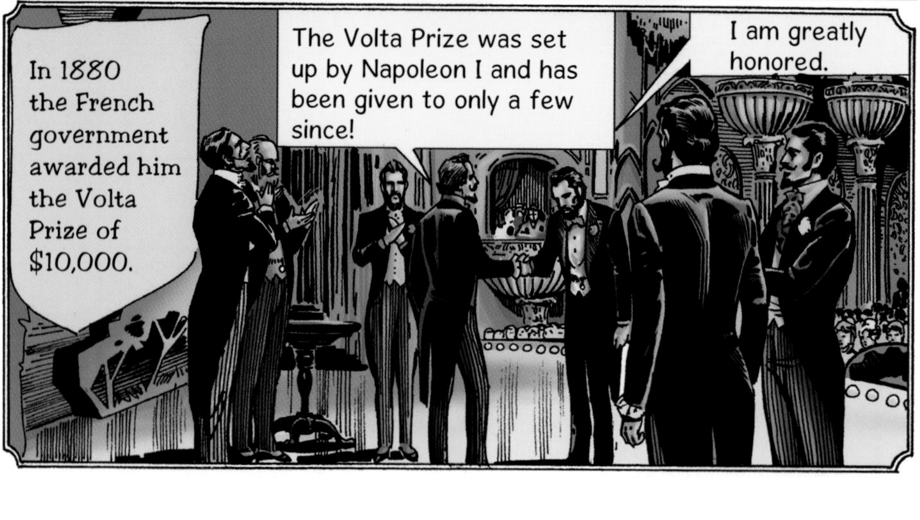
In 1880 the French government awarded him the Volta Prize of $10,000.
The Volta Prize was set up by Napoleon I and has been given to only a few since!
I am greatly honored.

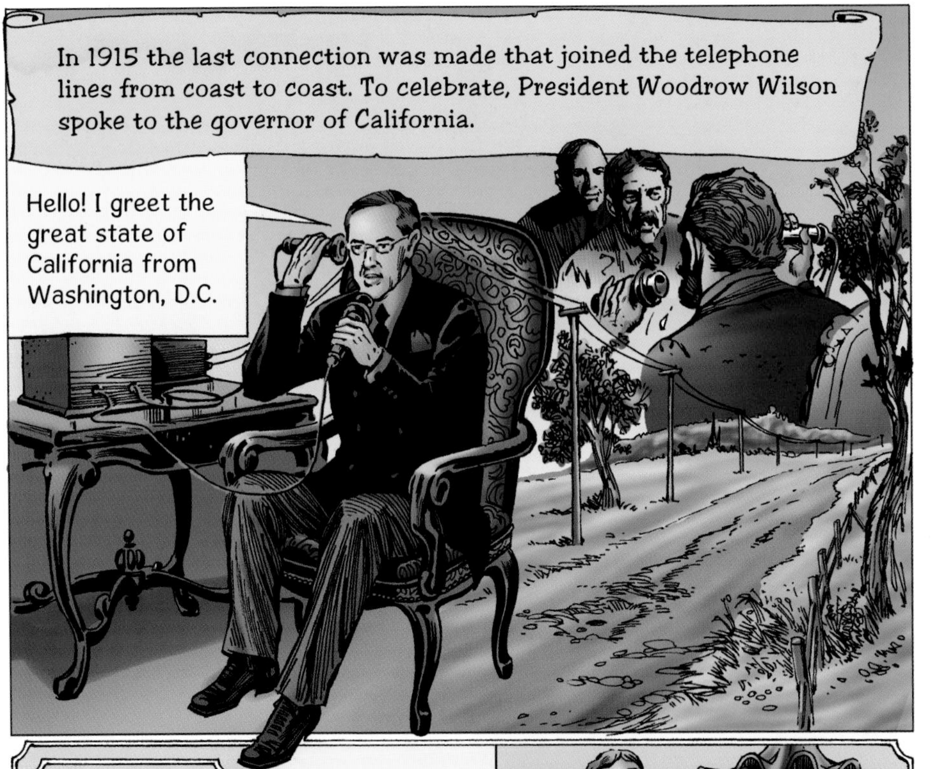
In 1915 the last connection was made that joined the telephone lines from coast to coast. To celebrate, President Woodrow Wilson spoke to the governor of California.
Hello! I greet the great state of California from Washington, D.C.

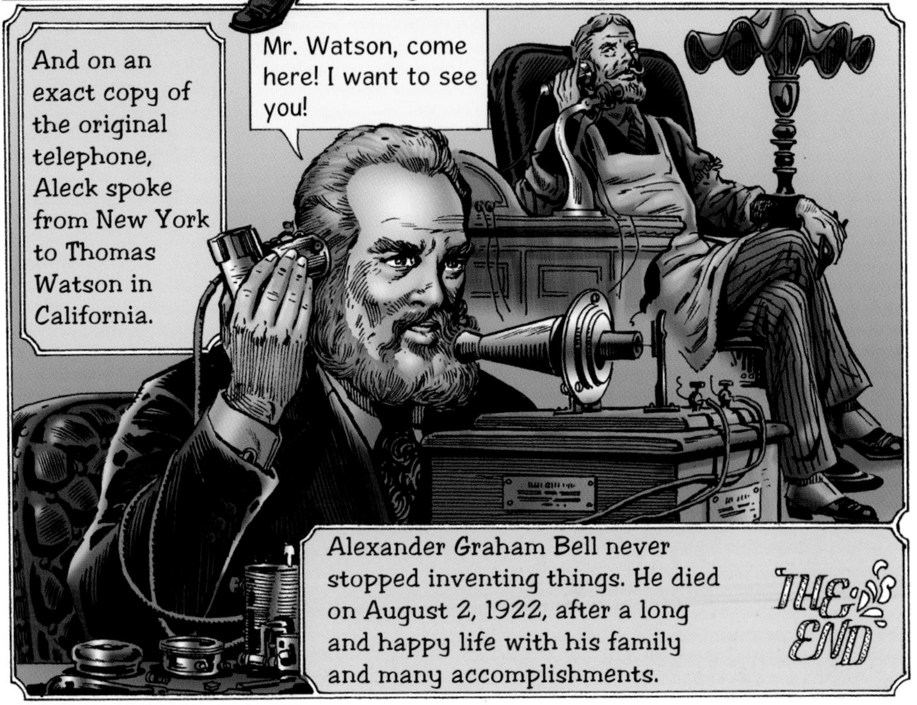
And on an exact copy of the original telephone, Aleck spoke from New York to Thomas Watson in California.
Mr. Watson, come here! I want to see you!
Alexander Graham Bell never stopped inventing things. He died on August 2, 1922, after a long and happy life with his family and many accomplishments.
THE END